The Decline and Fall of the Roman Empire

Titles in the World History Series

WORLD
HISTORY SERIES ■ ■ ■

The Decline and Fall of the Roman Empire

by
Don Nardo

Lucent Books, P.O. Box 289011, San Diego, CA 92198-9011

Library of Congress Cataloging-in-Publication Data

Nardo, Don, 1947–
    The decline and fall of the Roman Empire / by Don Nardo
       p. cm.—(World history series)
    Includes bibliographical references and index.
    Summary: Discusses the Roman Empire's rise to greatness
as well as its eventual decline and fall brought about by
increasingly dramatic military, economic, and social changes.
  ISBN 1-56006-314-9
    1. Rome—History—Empire, 30 B.C.–476 A.D.—Juvenile
literature.   2. Byzantine Empire—History—Juvenile
literature.   [1. Rome—History—Empire, 30 B.C.–476 A.D.]
I. Title. II. Series.
DG311.N265   1998
937'.06—dc21   97–49334
                                       CIP
                                       AC

Contents

Foreword

Each year on the first day of school, nearly every history teacher faces the task of explaining why his or her students should study history. One logical answer to this question is that exploring what happened in our past explains how the things we often take for granted—our customs, ideas, and institutions—came to be. As statesman and historian Winston Churchill put it, "Every nation or group of nations has its own tale to tell. Knowledge of the trials and struggles is necessary to all who would comprehend the problems, perils, challenges, and opportunities which confront us today." Thus, a study of history puts modern ideas and institutions in perspective. For example, though the founders of the United States were talented and creative thinkers, they clearly did not invent the concept of democracy. Instead, they adapted some democratic ideas that had originated in ancient Greece and with which the Romans, the British, and others had experimented. An exploration of these cultures, then, reveals their very real connection to us through institutions that continue to shape our daily lives.

Another reason often given for studying history is the idea that lessons exist in the past from which contemporary societies can benefit and learn. This idea, although controversial, has always been an intriguing one for historians. Those who agree that society can benefit from the past often quote philosopher George Santayana's famous statement, "Those who cannot remember the past are condemned to repeat it." Historians who ascribe to Santayana's philosophy believe that, for

example, studying the events that led up to the major world wars or other significant historical events would allow society to chart a different and more favorable course in the future.

Just as difficult as convincing students to realize the importance of studying history is the search for useful and interesting supplementary materials that present historical events in a context that can be easily understood. The volumes in Lucent Books' World History Series attempt to present a broad, balanced, and penetrating view of the march of history. Ancient Egypt's important wars and rulers, for example, are presented against the rich and colorful backdrop of Egyptian religious, social, and cultural developments. The series engages the reader by enhancing historical events with these cultural contexts. For example, in *Ancient Greece*, the text covers the role of women in that society. Slavery is discussed in *The Roman Empire*, as well as how slaves earned their freedom. The numerous and varied aspects of everyday life in these and other societies are explored in each volume of the series. Additionally, the series covers the major political, cultural, and philosophical ideas as the torch of civilization is passed from ancient Mesopotamia and Egypt, through Greece, Rome, Medieval Europe, and other world cultures, to the modern day.

The material in the series is formatted in a thorough, precise, and organized manner. Each volume offers the reader a comprehensive and clearly written overview of an important historical event or period. The topic under discussion is placed in a broad historical context. For example, *The Italian Renaissance* begins with a discussion of the High Middle Ages and the loss of central control that allowed certain Italian cities to develop artistically. The book ends by looking forward to the Reformation and interpreting the societal changes that grew out of the Renaissance. Thus, students are not only involved in an historical era, but also enveloped by the events leading up to that era and the events following it.

One important and unique feature in the World History Series is the primary and secondary source quotations that richly supplement each volume. These quotes are useful in a number of ways. First, they allow students access to sources they would not normally be exposed to because of the difficulty and obscurity of the original source. The quotations range from interesting anecdotes to farsighted cultural perspectives and are drawn from historical witnesses both past and present. Second, the quotes demonstrate how and where historians themselves derive their information on the past as they strive to reach a consensus on historical events. Lastly, all of the quotes are footnoted, familiarizing students with the citation process and allowing them to verify quotes and/or look up the original source if the quote piques their interest.

Finally, the books in the World History Series provide a detailed launching point for further research. Each book contains a bibliography specifically geared toward student research. A second, annotated bibliography introduces students to all the sources the author consulted when compiling the book. A chronology of important dates gives students an overview, at a glance, of the topic covered. Where applicable, a glossary of terms is included.

In short, the series is designed not only to acquaint readers with the basics of history, but also to make them aware that their lives are a part of an ongoing human saga. Perhaps they will then come to the same realization as famed historian Arnold Toynbee. In his monumental work, *A Study of History,* he wrote about becoming aware of history flowing through him in a mighty current, and of his own life "welling like a wave in the flow of this vast tide."

Important Dates in the Decline and Fall of the Roman Empire

B.C.	509	44	31	30	27	A.D.	98	180	193	212	235	284	293	307	312

B.C.

509
The leading Roman landowners throw out their last king and establish the Roman Republic.

44
After declaring himself "dictator for life," politician and military general Julius Caesar is assassinated by a group of disgruntled senators, pushing the Roman world, already exhausted from a recent series of horrendous civil wars, toward more chaos and bloodshed.

31
In the Republic's last power struggle, Caesar's adopted son, Octavian, defeats his last rivals at Actium, in western Greece, and gains firm control of the Mediterranean world.

27
With the blessings of the Senate, Octavian takes the name of Augustus. Historians usually mark this date as the beginning of the Roman Empire, with Augustus as its first emperor (although he himself never used that title, preferring to call himself "first citizen").

ca. 30 B.C–A.D. 180
The approximate years of the so-called *Pax Romana,* a period in which the Mediterranean world under the first several Roman emperors enjoys relative peace and prosperity.

A.D.

98–117
Reign of the emperor Trajan, in which the Roman Empire reaches its greatest size and power.

180
Death of the emperor Marcus Aurelius, marking the end of the *Pax Romana* era and the beginning of Rome's steady slide into economic and political crisis and eventually near anarchy.

193–235
Period of the combined reigns of the emperors of the Severan dynasty, beginning with Septimius Severus and ending with Alexander Severus.

212
Caracalla, Septimius Severus's son, extends citizenship rights to all free adult males in the Empire.

235–284
The Empire suffers under the strain of terrible political upheaval and civil strife, prompting later historians to call the third century Rome's "century of crisis" or "the anarchy."

284
Diocletian becomes emperor and initiates sweeping political, economic, and social reforms, in effect reconstructing the Empire under a new blueprint.

293
Diocletian establishes the first Tetrarchy, a power-sharing arrangement in which two emperors (with the title of Augustus) reign, one in the east, the other in the west, each with an assistant (with the title of Caesar).

307–337
Reign of the emperor Constantine I, who carries on the reforms begun by Diocletian.

312
Constantine defeats his rival, the usurper Maxentius, at Rome's Milvian Bridge.

313

Constantine and his eastern colleague, Licinius, issue the so-called Edict of Milan, granting religious toleration to the formerly hated and persecuted Christians.

330

Constantine founds the city of Constantinople on the Bosporus Strait, making it the capital of the eastern section of the Empire.

361–363

Reign of the emperor Julian, a brilliant and capable individual who, in the face of Christianity's growing popularity, tries but fails to reestablish paganism as Rome's dominant religion.

ca. 370

The Huns, a savage nomadic people from central Asia, sweep into eastern Europe, pushing the Goths and other "barbarian" peoples into the northern Roman provinces.

378

The eastern emperor Valens is disastrously defeated by the Visigoths at Adrianople.

395

The emperor Theodosius I dies, leaving his sons Arcadius and Honorius in control of a permanently divided Roman Empire.

ca. 407

As Rome steadily loses control of several of its northern and western provinces, Britain falls under the sway of barbarian tribes.

410

The Visigoths, led by Alaric, sack Rome.

451

After terrorizing and pillaging Roman lands for more than a decade, Attila, war chief of the Huns, is defeated by a combined army of Romans and barbarian federates at Chalons, in what is now northern France.

455

Rome is sacked again, this time by the Vandals, led by Gaiseric.

476

The German-born general Odoacer demands that the emperor, the young Romulus Augustulus, grant him and his men federate status; when the emperor refuses, Odoacer deposes him. Later historians came to see this removal of the last Roman emperor as the "fall" of Rome, although Roman life went on more or less as usual for some time under Odoacer and other barbarian rulers.

493

Theodoric the Ostrogoth seizes power from Odoacer.

527–565

Reign of the eastern emperor Justinian I, who attempts to regain some of the western Roman lands lost to the barbarians.

568

Another barbarian tribe, the Lombards, takes control of northern and central Italy. Hereafter, eastern and western Rome have little contact.

1453

The Ottoman Turks besiege, sack, and seize control of Constantinople, marking the end of the last remnant of the Roman Empire.

Descent into the Kingdom of Rust

One day late in the summer of A.D. 476, a stalwart man of Germanic birth named Odoacer, formerly an army general of the western Roman Empire, led a column of his troops into Ravenna, the northern Italian town then serving as the western imperial capital. Odoacer's men had just proclaimed him "king" of Italy. Using this authority (which though illegal was sufficiently well backed by military power), Odoacer proceeded, without striking a blow, to order the terrified young emperor, Romulus Augustulus, off the throne. According to an anonymous sixth-century chronicler, "Odoacer deposed Augustulus but granted him his life, pitying his infancy and because he was comely, and he gave him an income . . . and sent him to live . . . with his relatives."[1] No emperor took the boy's place, and many later scholars came to view this event as the fall of the western Roman Empire.

The end of the western Empire marked much more than just the demise of a particular regime, form of government, or localized society. What was passing away in the late fifth and early sixth centuries was the remnant of a once awesomely powerful, widely influential, and culturally magnificent civilization. "Human history shows no more brilliant example of success in statesmanship than the Roman Empire," remarks classical scholar Mortimer Chambers. "It united the entire civilized portion of the West [that is, the lands west of the Near East; essentially speaking, Europe] . . . under a single dominion for more than two centuries. This achievement has never been approached by any later state."[2]

It must also be stressed that it was more than just the Empire, founded in 27 B.C. by the first Roman emperor, Augustus Caesar, that was expiring; the Empire was a continuation of the stately and vigorous Roman Republic, established in 509 B.C.; and the Republic itself had supplanted a long line of kings stretching back to the eighth century B.C. Rome, the so-called eternal city, had endured, prospered, and in many ways decided the fate of the Mediterranean world for more than twelve centuries. Thus, powerless and pathetic as he may have been in that fading twilight of Roman power, poor Augustulus was the heir to a very ancient and long-lived, as well as grand, civilization. The passing of so important a civilization, Chambers maintains, "must rank as one of the greatest historical turning points in man's long story."[3] Indeed, historians generally view western Rome's disintegration as the end of ancient times, or antiquity, and beginning of medieval times, often called the Middle Ages. It was during the Middle Ages that the primitive kingdoms that grew upon the wreckage of the western Empire evolved into the precursors of the nations of modern Europe.

The Consensus of Scholarship

Not surprisingly, so epic a turning point as Rome's demise has long attracted the attention of scholars and ordinary readers alike, all asking why and how did it occur? What caused Roman civilization to decline? And at what point in Rome's history did that decline begin? The first major modern study that attempted to answer these questions was *The Decline and Fall of the Roman Empire,* published in six volumes between 1776 and 1788 by the great English historian Edward Gibbon. This huge intellectual accomplishment, still considered the masterwork of its field, eventually delineated four major causes for Rome's decline and fall. These were its "immoderate greatness," or its having become too large and complex to govern itself efficiently and safely; too much indulgence (by upper-class Romans) in wealth and luxury at the expense of the state; the devastating invasions of northern European Germanic tribes, whom the Romans referred to as "barbarians"; and the rise of Christianity, whose ideas supposedly weakened Rome's traditional martial spirit.

Since Gibbon's time, many historians have agreed or disagreed with his conclusions, and the literature exploring Rome's fall has been large (literally thousands of books and articles), rich, inventive, and both thought- and debate-provoking. The blame for the fall has been placed on such diverse causes as climatic changes that brought about a decline in agriculture, class wars between the poor and privileged, depopulation as the result of plagues and wars, race mixture with "inferior" peoples, the moral and economic ravages of slavery, and brain damage from lead poisoning, to name only a few. Some, like Gibbon, have suggested multiple causes. "The process of decline was due not to a single cause," writes historian Solomon Katz, "but to a variety of interacting factors—political, economic, social, cultural, and psychological."[4]

Presently, at the transition from the twentieth century to the twenty-first, the overall consensus of scholarship about Rome's demise falls into two broad camps. The first sees the decline and fall as mainly military in nature (while acknowledging that other factors were involved in lesser degrees), the result of the accumulative effects of one devastating barbarian incursion after another in the Empire's final century. For a brief summary, no one has managed to improve on Gibbon: "The endless column of barbarians pressed on the Roman Empire with accumulated weight; and if the foremost were destroyed, the vacant space was instantly replenished by new assailants."[5] In his modern classic, *History of the Later Roman Empire* (1923), the late J. B. Bury refined this view, suggesting that the destruction was gradual and "the consequence of *a series of contingent events,*"[6] that is, one unexpected and debilitating military/political incident leading to another and eventually creating an overall downward spiral. More recent scholars have provided new insights about the steady fragmentation of the Empire in the barbarians' wake and have also shown how, during this period, the Roman army grew increasingly weaker, less disciplined, and thereby less capable of stopping the invaders.

The other scholarly camp (which does not necessarily argue with or refute the first) suggests that in a way Rome did not fall in the fifth century. These historians instead emphasize the continuity of Roman institutions, culture, and ideas. They point out, on the one hand, that the eastern Roman realm based at Constantinople, which became the Byzantine Empire, survived the western realm by nearly a thousand years. On the other hand, they say, western Roman culture gradually, rather than catastrophically, was transformed into what we call medieval European civilization. The classic recent work in this vein is Peter Brown's *The World of Late Antiquity* (1971). Through such continuity, it is believed, Roman language,

ideas, laws, and so on survived to make the modern world what it is. This fact, by itself, is certainly an important enough motive for people today to look back at and examine Rome and its fall from power.

An Evolving Imperial System

Depending on which cause or causes for Rome's decline they advocate, scholars differ on the starting dates for that decline, for the beginning of what has come to be called the "Later Roman Empire." This is a sticky problem. Despite the tendency of many historians to portray the Later Empire overall as a period of decay, Rome's decline was not a simple, steady downswing beginning at point A and ending conveniently at point B. For instance, Rome suffered significant deterioration when it fell into near anarchy in the third century, yet it bounced back in an amazing

Among the so-called barbarians who overwhelmed Rome in its final years were the Franks, here depicted during their invasion of Gaul.

In this relief from the famous column of the second-century A.D. emperor Trajan, Roman soldiers attack a German fortress. Over the course of succeeding centuries, it became more common for Germans to attack Roman fortresses.

display of resiliency in the early fourth century, thanks in large degree to the reforms and strong leadership of the emperors Diocletian and Constantine. Hence, it is more accurate to describe the crisis of the third century, the fourth-century revival, and other later imperial trends, in the words of the brilliant modern Roman scholar Averil Cameron, as temporary phases "in a developing and evolving imperial system."[7]

During the decades that followed the death of the last of the so-called good emperors, Marcus Aurelius in the late second century, the Empire began to experience increasingly dramatic military, economic, and social changes; eventually, these changes would transform it into a new, and for a time still impressive, but decidedly less secure and happy place in which to live. Ironically, we need not rely on modern studies to tell us that Aurelius's passing was an ominous watershed. After this fateful juncture, the second-century historian Dio Cassius astutely observed, "Our history now descends from a kingdom of gold to one of iron and rust, as the affairs of the Romans then did."[8]

1 From Obscurity to Mediterranean Mastery: Rome's Rise to Greatness

For a mighty nation or empire to decline and fall, it must first undergo an auspicious rise to power and ascendancy. And so it was with Rome, whose inhabitants rose slowly but relentlessly from obscure and lowly circumstances to the overlordship of the known world. The early Romans evolved from one of a group of Latin-speaking tribes that descended from central Europe into Italy beginning about 2000 B.C. By about the year 1000, the semi-nomadic Romans began to settle down, establishing villages on seven low hills at a bend in the Tiber River on the northern edge of the fertile plain of Latium. This plain was bordered on the west by the Mediterranean Sea and on the east by the rugged Apennine Mountains, which run north-south through the Italian "boot." Modern scholars are unsure about the exact location and date of the original settlement that would later become the most powerful city in the Mediterranean-European sphere. However, as British historian Anthony Kamm explains:

> The Romans themselves were in no doubt when Rome was founded: 21 April 753 B.C. On that day of the year, too, they celebrated the traditional festival of the Parilia in honor of Pales, the god . . . of shepherds and sheep. In

1948 traces were found on the Palatine Hill, the central and most easily fortified of the seven hills of the ultimate city, of the huts of a settlement of shepherd folk dating from about 750 B.C. Current excavations have uncovered the remains of a ritual boundary wall of about the same period.[9]

Monarchy Gives Way to Republic

At first, these hardy shepherds and farmers who called themselves Romans lived a rustic, uncultured existence, dwelling in timber shacks with thatched roofs. By the eighth century B.C., however, living conditions for many Romans improved. Archaeological evidence, writes noted scholar T. J. Cornell, "points to an increase in the general level of wealth and prosperity. There must have been a rise in productivity, caused at least in part by improved agricultural techniques."[10] Ruled by a series of kings, Rome grew steadily from a group of crude villages to a small city, complete with stone sewers and public buildings. Most imposing of all was the first of Rome's temples to its chief god, Jupiter, the construction of which, the first-century Roman historian

Livy tells us, was supervised by King Tarquinius Superbus.

Builders and engineers were brought in from all over Etruria, and the project involved the use not only of public funds but also of a large number of [Roman] laborers from the poorer classes. The work was hard in itself,

and came in addition to their regular military duties; but it was an honorable burden with a solemn religious significance, and they were not, on the whole, unwilling to bear it.[11]

Not long after the completion of the temple, the tough-minded, aggressive, and independent Romans showed that

Romulus Founds Rome

According to Rome's most popular legend, the city was established in 753 B.C. by a young man named Romulus shortly after the death of his brother Remus. This excerpt from the first-century A.D. Greek historian Plutarch's Life of Romulus *(from his famous* Parallel Lives*) describes how the initial foundations of the city were supposedly laid.*

"Romulus, having buried his brother Remus . . . set to building his city; and sent for men out of Tuscany [then Etruria, homeland of the Etruscans], who directed him . . . in all the ceremonies to be observed, as in a religious rite. First, they dug a round trench . . . and into it solemnly threw the first-fruits of all things either good by custom or necessary by nature. . . . Making this trench . . . their center, they laid out the boundary of the city in a circle around it. Then the founder [Romulus] fitted to a plow a metal plowshare [blade], and, yoking together a bull and a cow, drove himself a deep line or furrow round the boundary. . . . With this line they laid out the [city] wall; and where they designed to make a gate, there they . . . left a space. . . . As for the day they began to build the city, it is universally agreed to have been the twenty-first of April, and that day the Romans annually keep holy, calling it their country's birthday."

Since no one knew what Romulus looked like, this later Roman likeness of him is purely fanciful.

what they were *not* willing to bear was the continued rule of the monarchy. In about 509 B.C., the city's leading citizens, the well-to-do landholding patricians, organized a bold rebellion. When news of the uprising reached Superbus, Livy wrote, "the king immediately started for Rome, to restore order. . . . Tarquin found the city gates shut against him and his exile decreed."[12]

Their victory complete, the rebels proceeded to establish their own national state, the Roman Republic. The new re-publican government was run by representatives of the people, although Roman leaders at first defined "the people" rather narrowly. Only free adult males who owned weapons (and were therefore eligible for military service), a group that made up a minority of the population, could vote or hold public office. Some of these citizens met periodically in a body called the Assembly, which proposed and voted on new laws and also annually elected two consuls, or administrator-generals, to run the state and lead the army. In his *Laws*,

This undated copper engraving, probably from the nineteenth century, depicts a session of the early Roman Senate, the most powerful republican political institution.

the great first-century B.C. orator and statesman Marcus Tullius Cicero would later describe these leaders and the special office of dictator, which was to be filled in a national emergency:

> There shall be two magistrates with royal powers. . . . They shall be called consuls. In the field they shall hold the supreme military power and shall be subject to no one. The safety of the people shall be their highest law. . . . But when a serious war or civil dissensions arise, one man shall hold, for not longer than six months, the power which ordinarily belongs to the two consuls. . . . And after being appointed under favorable auspices, he shall be master of the people.[13]

The other legislative body, the Senate, was composed exclusively of patricians, who held their positions for life. Although in theory the senators were mere governmental advisers, in reality they usually dictated the policies of the consuls and, through the use of wealth and high position, indirectly influenced the way the members of the Assembly voted. Thus, except under extreme circumstances, the Senate held the real power in republican Rome.

Belief in a Greater Destiny

Yet in an age when kings and other absolute monarchs ruled almost everywhere else in the known world, the Roman Republic was a very progressive and enlightened political entity indeed. Though most Romans did not have a say in state policy, many had a measurable voice in choosing leaders and making laws. And these laws often offered an umbrella of protection for members of all classes against the arbitrary abuses of potentially corrupt leaders. "Law is the bond which secures these our privileges in the commonwealth [empire]," Cicero would later write, "the foundation of our . . . liberty, the fountainhead [main source] of justice. Within the law are reposed the mind and heart, the judgment and conviction of the state."[14] For these and other reasons, republican government proved increasingly flexible and largely met the needs of Romans of all classes.

The result was that the Roman people came to view their system with great pride and patriotism. In time they came to believe that the rise of that system and indeed the very founding of Rome centuries earlier were not chance events; rather, the gods had blessed these national beginnings and ordained that the Romans, the master race, were destined to rule over others. This belief in a greater destiny fueled the first stages of Roman expansion. In the fifth century B.C., Roman armies began marching outward from Latium and subduing neighboring peoples, including their northern neighbors, the Etruscans, whose main stronghold of Veii was captured circa 396 B.C. In the decades that followed, many other towns and peoples of central Italy became incorporated into the growing Roman sphere. By the early third century, after Rome's defeat of the Samnites, a powerful and much-feared hill people, Roman territory had expanded to cover some fifty thousand square miles, three times its original size.

Much of the success of these early conquests was the result of the Romans' gift for political conciliation and organization. Instead of taking vengeance on and treating former enemies harshly, they opted for

The fortress of the city of Veii, the main stronghold of the Etruscans. The Etruscans inhabited the region north of Rome, then called Etruria and now Tuscany, both terms deriving from the name of the people.

the wiser and more fruitful approach of making treaties with them and granting them Roman citizenship and legal privileges. They also initiated the habit of introducing the Latin language, as well as Roman ideas, laws, and customs, to non-Latin peoples, in a sense "Romanizing" them. "What made the Romans so remarkable," comments noted classical scholar Michael Grant,

> was a talent for patient political reasonableness that was unique in the ancient world. . . . On the whole, Rome found it advisable . . . to keep its bargains with its allies, displaying a self-restraint, a readiness to compromise, and a calcu-

lated generosity that the world had never seen. And so the allies, too, had little temptation to feel misused. The proud Samnites, it is true, had lost a considerable amount of their land to Roman settlers. . . . But they were only a few out of a grand total of one hundred and twenty Italian communities with which Rome, in due course, formed perpetual alliances. After the end of the Samnite wars [about 290 B.C.] a network of such agreements was extended across the whole of central Italy.[15]

This rather lenient and very efficient method of administration made it easier for Rome to solidify its gains and continue to expand, since it often instilled in former adversaries some degree of gratitude and in some cases even a sense of loyalty to Rome. Describing this brand of devotion, Cicero later wrote:

> Every citizen of a corporate town [one annexed by Rome] has, I take it, two fatherlands, that of which he is a native, and that of which he is a citizen. I will never deny my allegiance to my native town, only I will never forget that Rome is my greater Fatherland, and that my native town is but a portion of Rome.[16]

Phenomenal Success at a Price

The conquest of central Italy did not satisfy Rome's growing appetite for territory and power. In the late 280s B.C. the Romans turned on the numerous Greek cities that had sprung up across southern Italy in the preceding few centuries and in the space of two decades absorbed them, becoming the undisputed masters of all Italy south of the Po Valley, the northern region at the foot of the Alps. Next, Rome cast its gaze beyond the shores of Italy and onto neighboring Mediterranean coasts. Carthage, a powerful trading city and empire centered at the northern tip of Tunisia, on the African coast, fell to Roman steel after the three devastating Punic Wars, fought between 264 and 146 B.C.[17] As prizes, Rome gained the large and fertile island of Sicily at the foot of the Italian boot, other western Mediterranean islands, Spain, and much of northern Africa.

Rome had originally been strictly a land power; however, out of necessity dur-ing the Punic conflicts, it built a powerful navy. Soon after obliterating Carthage, it unleashed its formidable combined land and naval forces on the Greek kingdoms clustered in the Mediterranean's eastern sphere, including Macedonia, Seleucia, and Egypt. By the end of the second century B.C., the Mediterranean had become, in effect, a Roman lake; in fact, thereafter the Romans rather arrogantly referred to that waterway as *mare nostrum*, "our sea."

But Rome's phenomenal success had come at a price. By the dawn of the first century B.C., ominous cracks had appeared in the Republic's structure. First, in their rise to Mediterranean mastery, the Romans had found it increasingly difficult to administer so many diverse lands and peoples with a governmental system that had been designed to rule a single people inhabiting a small city-state. Also, conquest and rule required large, well-disciplined armies and able generals, both of which, of course, Rome had in abundance. But the state's policy, an unwise one it turned out, was not to reward its soldiers with pensions and land when they retired. Meeting this need, the wealthiest and most powerful generals began using their influence to secure such benefits for their men. Consequently, the troops began to show more allegiance to their generals than to the state. They served these leaders, the second-century A.D. Greek historian Appian wrote,

> not by the force of laws, but by reason of private promises, not against the common enemy but against private foes, not against foreigners, but against fellow-citizens. . . . All this relaxed military discipline, and the soldiers thought that they were not so much serving in the army as lending

assistance . . . to leaders who needed them for their own personal ends.[18]

The "personal ends" of these generals increasingly consisted of amassing great political power and challenging the government's authority. Among the most successful were Cornelius Sulla, the first Roman consul to seize the capital by force; Gnaeus Pompey, who won lasting fame after ridding the Mediterranean of pirates; Julius Caesar, who conquered the wild lands of Gaul, what is now France and Belgium, and met a violent end at the hands of senatorial assassins in 44 B.C.; and Mark Antony, Caesar's protégé, famous for his love affair and alliance with Egypt's Queen Cleopatra. These and other contenders for state power met head-on in a series of horrendously destructive civil wars that killed hundreds of thousands of people and brought the Republic and its ideals of representative government crashing down. Cicero, the last great republican champion, quite literally lost his head, the victim of Antony's henchmen.

The Romans Defeat the Greeks

This tract from Livy's massive history of Rome graphically illustrates the formidable qualities of the Roman armies that conquered the Mediterranean. Described is the bloody conclusion of the Battle of Pydna, fought in Greece in 168 B.C., the final conflict of the Third Macedonian War. Afterward, the victorious Romans dismantled the Macedonian kingdom, bringing its parts into their expanding Empire.

"While the general slaughter of the Macedonian infantry was going on, except for those who flung away their arms and fled, the cavalry withdrew from the battle almost unscathed. The [Macedonian] king [Perseus] himself was the leader of the flight. . . . For a long time the phalanx [the Greek battle formation] was cut to pieces from the front, the flanks [sides], and the rear. In the end, those who had slipped from the hands of the Romans fled to the sea without their weapons, and some even went into the water, raising their hands to the men on board the [Roman] ships and begging humbly for their lives. . . . But when they were ruthlessly slaughtered from the boats, those who could made for the shore again by swimming, where they met with destruction in a more horrible shape; for the [battle] elephants, driven to the shore by their drivers, trampled down the men as they came out of the water and crushed them to death. It is readily agreed that the Romans never killed so many Macedonians in one battle; in fact about 20,000 men were slain, about 6,000 . . . were taken alive, and 5,000 scattered fugitives were captured. Of the victors, not more than a hundred fell."

Romans are pitted against one another in the terrible bloodbath accompanying Sulla's assault on the capital.

The Blessings of Peace

From this long and destructive orgy of personal ambition and civil strife, one man finally emerged victorious—Octavian, Caesar's adopted son. Soon after the defeat of his last rivals, Antony and Cleopatra, in a large naval battle near the Greek town of Actium in 31 B.C., the Senate, now virtually powerless, conferred on Octavian the title of Augustus, "the exalted one." He immediately began building a new, more autocratic Roman state on the wreckage of the now defunct Republic. Though he never personally used the title of emperor, he was in fact the first ruler of the political unit that became known as the Roman Empire.

Augustus and most of his immediate successors were thoughtful, effective rulers who brought prosperity and peace to the Roman world;[19] consequently, the period of their combined reigns, lasting from about 30 B.C. to A.D. 180, became known as the *Pax Romana,* or "Great Roman Peace." The five emperors who ruled from 96 to 180—Nerva, Trajan, Hadrian, Antoninus Pius, and Marcus Aurelius—were particularly capable and enlightened (hence the nickname later accorded them—the "five good emperors"). They brought Roman civilization to its political, economic, and

Increasing Disloyalty in the Ranks

In this excerpt from his Civil Wars, *the second-century* A.D. *Greek historian Appian attempts to explain the increasing insubordination, desertions, and disloyalty to the state of large numbers of Roman soldiers in the fateful first century* B.C.

"The cause was that the generals for the most part, as is usually the case in civil wars, were not regularly chosen; that their armies were not drawn from the enrollment according to the ancestral custom nor for the benefit of their country; that they did not serve the public, but rather those alone who brought them together; and that they served these not by the force of laws, but by reason of private promises, not against the common enemy, but against private foes, not against foreigners, but against fellow citizens, their equals in rank. All this relaxed military discipline, and the soldiers thought that they were not so much serving in the army as lending assistance, by their own favor and judgment, to leaders who needed them for their own personal ends. Desertion, which had formerly been unpardonable to Romans, was now actually rewarded with gifts; whole armies resorted to it, and also a number of illustrious men. . . . The common pretense of the generals that they were all striving for the good of the country made desertion easier, in the thought that one could serve his country in any party. Understanding these facts, the generals tolerated this behavior, for they knew that their authority over their armies depended on donatives [personal gifts] rather than on law."

cultural zenith, prompting Edward Gibbon's later famous remark:

> If a man were called upon to fix the period in the history of the world during which the condition of the human race was most happy and prosperous, he would without hesitation name that which elapsed from the accession of Nerva to the death of Aurelius. . . . Their united reigns are possibly the only period of history in which the happiness of a great people was the sole object of government.[20]

Under Trajan, an able, thoughtful, and generous ruler, the Empire was larger than it had ever been or ever would be. It stretched from the Atlantic Ocean in the west to the Persian Gulf in the east, and from northern Africa in the south to central Britain in the north, a colossal political unit encompassing some 3.5 million square miles and 100 million people. Hadrian,

This famous statue, showing Augustus wearing an ornately embossed breastplate, was discovered at Prima Porta, near Rome.

like Trajan, devoted all of his energies to running a fair and efficient government. Among Hadrian's humane accomplishments were an expansion of the Roman welfare system, the creation of free schools for poor children, and the strengthening of laws protecting slaves from abuse. His successor, Antoninus Pius, was so ethical, honest, and sincere that his first official act as emperor was to donate his large personal fortune to the public treasury; he ran the economy so well that at the end of his reign the state enjoyed a gigantic cash surplus. Thus, when Marcus Aurelius took the throne on Antoninus's passing in 161, their contemporary the Greek writer Aelius Aristides hardly exaggerated in his praise of the Roman achievement: "Every place is full of gymnasia, fountains, gateways, temples, shops, and schools. . . . Only those outside your Empire, if there are any, are fit to be pitied for losing such blessings. . . . You

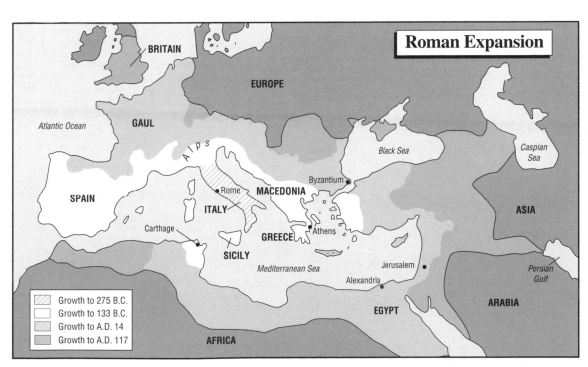

Roman Expansion

BRITAIN

EUROPE

Atlantic Ocean

GAUL

Alps

SPAIN

Rome

ITALY

MACEDONIA

Byzantium

Black Sea

Caspian Sea

ASIA

Carthage

SICILY

GREECE

Athens

Mediterranean Sea

Jerusalem

Alexandria

Persian Gulf

EGYPT

ARABIA

AFRICA

Growth to 275 B.C.
Growth to 133 B.C.
Growth to A.D. 14
Growth to A.D. 117

have surveyed the whole world . . . and civilized it all with system and order." [21]

Unbeknownst to the new emperor and his largely happy subjects, however, Rome's great era of peace and plenty was about to end. The specters of war, disease, political instability, economic decline, and social unrest were massing for a combined assault, the effects of which would reach a ruinous crescendo in the coming century. Aurelius was as hardworking, just, and honest a ruler as has ever lived. But he had no power to stop, nor was he likely even aware of, the mass migrations of Germanic tribes through northern Europe that would soon send barbarian hordes spilling over Roman borders; nor had he any control over the spread of a deadly plague brought back to Italy by soldiers returning from a Near Eastern campaign; nor can he be held responsible for the incompetence, greed, dishonesty, and brutality of his successors. In the years following his passing, for the first time in living memory, large numbers of Romans felt uncertain about the future. That uncertainty would soon turn to trembling fear.

Chapter

2 To the Brink and Back: Weathering the Century of Crisis

The reigns of Marcus Aurelius, last of the so-called good emperors, and his immediate successors marked the transition from the peaceful and prosperous *Pax Romana* era to what historians variously call "the century of crisis," "the anarchy," "the military monarchy," and "the age of the soldier-emperors." Whatever one chooses to call it, in the turbulent third century, Rome experienced a severe crisis in which its political and economic stability was shattered; in fact, at times it appeared that the Empire might collapse from an inability to deal with a prolonged onslaught of serious external threats and internal problems.

The external threats included violations of the realm's northern borders by Germanic tribes and full-scale war with the new and militarily formidable Sassanian Persian Empire, formerly the Parthian realm, on its eastern border.[22] Among Rome's internal problems during the fateful third century was poor leadership. In contrast to the honest and able rulers of the second century, most of those that followed were ambitious, brutal, and/or incompetent. Another problem was a breakdown of military discipline, loyalty, and efficiency, as Roman armies frequently ran amok, choosing and disposing of emperors at will. As the generals fought one another, as well as foreign invaders, war and political instability disrupted trade, farming declined, and money steadily lost its value. As a result of these threats and problems, law and order often broke down, poverty grew, and life in the Empire became increasingly miserable, dangerous, and uncertain.

The Empire Exceptionally Vulnerable

Examining these striking contrasts between the Rome of the *Pax Romana* and that of the third century naturally raises the question of how a strong and stable empire could have undergone so extensive and rapid a decline. The answer has two dimensions. First, that this decline turned out to be temporary and did not bring about Rome's complete collapse attests to the considerable fortitude and resiliency of the economy, political and social institutions, and people under the early emperors. As noted historian Chester Starr puts it, by the dawn of the third century "the Empire had built up a great inherited store of physical capital and spiritual strength thanks to its unification and prosperity in the past 200 years."[23]

On the other hand, this prolonged state of prosperity and unity, one unprecedented in human history, had been possible because Rome had enjoyed a long vacation from the ravages of war, both civil and foreign. The economic and political stability of the Empire, classical scholar Charles Freeman comments,

> was very delicate. Above all, it depended on peace. The Empire was, in fact, exceptionally vulnerable to war and invasion. The defenses along its defended borders were not designed to withstand major attacks, while roads ran from them towards cities whose riches lay unprotected by walls. Its armies were by now accustomed to fixed bases and would take some time to deploy, especially if they had to be moved large distances. The subjects of the Empire had enjoyed relatively low levels of taxation for decades and the resources needed to meet a challenge could not be easily raised at short notice.[24]

That the Empire of Aurelius's time was both vulnerable and resilient is illustrated by the major events of his reign. In 161 the Parthians, who had a long-standing dispute with Rome over possession of Armenia and other Near Eastern territories, invaded some of Rome's eastern provinces. The Roman armies that met this threat were victorious; however, on returning to Italy in 166, the soldiers brought back a deadly plague, which killed tens of thousands of people over the course of a decade.

At the height of this crisis, large bands of Germanic tribesmen began raiding across the Danube frontier, the Empire's northern border.[25] In succeeding years some of these incursions penetrated deep into the Empire's heartlands; one group

A sketch depicts the equestrian statue of the emperor Marcus Aurelius, which long stood on the Capitoline Hill. Aurelius's left hand originally held a statue of the goddess Victory.

of invaders besieged Aquileia, in northeastern Italy, while another reached the outskirts of Athens, Greece. Despite manpower shortages resulting from the eastern campaign and plague, the emperor and his troops met the challenge and, in a series of dogged campaigns spanning a decade, drove the intruders back. When the dedicated Aurelius died in 180, the northern borders were once more intact. Dio Cassius later provided this fitting epitaph that captures the plight of a noble man and a great empire both struggling to deal with rapidly mounting problems:

> He did not meet with the good fortune that he deserved, for he was not strong in body and was involved in a multitude of troubles throughout practically his entire reign. But for my part, I admire him all the more for this very reason, that amid unusual and extraordinary difficulties he both survived himself and preserved the Empire.[26]

The Leadership Crisis

In spite of Aurelius's admirable efforts, Rome soon found that its "extraordinary difficulties" had only just begun. The first new crisis, one that would frequently plague the Empire for nearly a century, was poor leadership. Aurelius's son, Commodus, who ascended the throne in 180 at the age of eighteen or nineteen, possessed a character almost exactly opposite that of his father and other recent emperors. Vain, selfish, and spoiled, he often neglected his governmental responsibilities and spent large sums of public money on his own luxuries. A fourth-century chronicler captured the squalor of both Commodus's character and imperial court:

> He would drink till dawn and squander the resources of the Roman Empire. In the evening he flitted through the taverns to the brothels [houses of prostitution]. . . . Commodus . . . killed his sister Lucilla. . . . Then, having debauched [seduced] his other sisters . . . he even gave one of the concubines [mistresses] the name of his mother. His wife, whom he had caught in adultery, he drove out, then banished her, and subsequently killed her.[27]

As for his foreign policy, what little there was of it, Commodus reversed his father's policy of resisting the influx of barbarian tribes into the northern provinces. Unwilling to interrupt his pleasures in Rome with time-consuming military campaigns, the young emperor struck a deal with the tribes. In exchange for peace, he allowed some of their members to settle in the border provinces and even encouraged some thirteen thousand barbarians to enlist in the Roman army. This angered most generals and other high officials, who felt that Rome needed to ensure its future safety by keeping the barbarians out. Commodus also made enemies by maintaining a reign of terror in the capital. His spies were everywhere and he ordered hundreds of people executed for trivial offenses. Few if any were surprised or sorry when a palace assassination plot succeeded, ending his corrupt reign in 192.

Many Romans no doubt assumed that with the despot dead the Empire's leadership would settle back into the more stable and productive mode of the "good" emperors. But they were wrong. The five years following Commodus's passing witnessed a chaotic and bloody power struggle in which his immediate successors, Pertinax and Didius Julianus, reigned only three months and sixty-six days, respectively, before suffering the same fate he had. Then several army generals in various sectors of the Empire claimed the throne, each receiving the backing of his troops. The strongest of these contenders was Septimius Severus, who emerged victorious in 197.

The Shameless and Cruel Commodus

This excerpt from the so-called Augustan History *of an unknown fourth-century chronicler describes the infamous character of Commodus, Marcus Aurelius's son, whose corrupt reign marked the beginning of the Empire's slide into the troubled times of the third century.*

"Straight from his earliest boyhood he was base, shameless, cruel, lecherous, defiled of mouth too and debauched [corrupt], already adept at those arts which do not accord with the position of emperor. . . . He gave advance warning of his future cruelty in his twelfth year. . . . For when he happened to have taken a bath in rather tepid water, he ordered the bath-keeper to be cast into the furnace. . . . When [as an adult] he came back to Rome [from a military campaign] he celebrated a triumph [victory parade], with Saoterus his debaucher [seducer] placed behind him in the chariot. In the course of the triumphal procession Commodus several times turned his head and kissed him, quite openly."

This bust of the emperor Commodus, now in Rome's Capitoline Museum, shows him bearing the club and lion skin of the hero Hercules, with whom he identified himself in the later years of his reign.

This detail from the Arch of Septimius Severus, erected by the Senate in 203 to celebrate Severus's Parthian victories, shows Roman soldiers and Parthian prisoners.

The Severi

Severus was a stern, strong, and able general who managed to restore order and keep the barbarians on their own side of the northern border. But he had little understanding of the Empire's serious internal problems, which were steadily worsening. The economy had weakened over the preceding decades, due to such factors as declining population (partly attributable to the plague of the 160s); a reduction of agricultural output, causing sporadic food shortages and rising food prices in the cities;[28] a slowly diminishing volume of trade; and

perhaps most destructive of all—inflation caused by devaluation of the coinage. A growing lack of gold and silver had, over preceding decades, forced the government to mint coins containing cheaper alloys, and this made money worth less. The *denarius,* one of the most common Roman coins, for example, was worth only about one-fortieth as much in Marcus Aurelius's time as at the beginning of the *Pax Romana.*

Severus failed to solve any of these problems; instead, he actually made some of them worse. For instance, he ordered another decrease in the amount of silver in coins, which further devalued money. This not only hindered trade and decreased people's buying power but also made his expensive military reforms harder to implement. He increased the army's size to thirty-six legions (regiments of about five thousand men each) plus auxiliary troops, creating a force of perhaps four hundred thousand men, and also raised the soldiers' pay. His successors maintained these large forces, while money became increasingly worthless; the result was that the next six decades saw the military pay and supply system buckle and finally break down.

An ardent and adamant militarist to the end, Severus is famous for the advice he gave his sons, Caracalla and Geta, on his deathbed in 211: "Enrich the soldiers, scorn everybody else."[29] For the most part, they and the other Severi, or members of Severus's dynasty, who held sway over Rome until 235, followed this shortsighted counsel. Caracalla, Severus's immediate successor, was a poor administrator who often treated his subjects cruelly.[30] To bolster his image, in 212 he made a huge show of granting citizenship to all free inhabitants of the realm, but this move was designed mainly to increase the number of people he could tax. Murdered by one of his own bodyguards in 217, Caracalla was succeeded by Macrinus (who probably helped engineer the assassination plot), Elagabalus, and Alexander Severus. All were ineffective rulers and ended up being assassinated or removed from power.

Foreign Invaders

The weakness and instability of Roman leadership under the later Severi, as well as the problems they faced, proved merely a foretaste of what followed them. For the next half century the Empire was threatened by invaders from the north and east, while the government was often in a state of turmoil or outright civil war. Trade continued to decline, money became almost totally worthless, many soldiers, unable to rely on government pay, looted at will, and poverty and crime were rampant. Between 235 and 284 more than fifty rulers, most of them generals backed by their troops, claimed the throne. Although about half of them were formally acknowledged as emperors, perhaps only eighteen had any legitimate claim. Their average reign was two and a half years, and all but one died by assassination or other violent means.

It was foolhardy and self-defeating, of course, for Roman rulers and generals to fight one another while they tried to beat back foreign invaders. But this is precisely what they did, and the Empire paid a terrible price in death, ruin, and misery. The first series of invasions came in the 230s as German tribes renewed their attacks on the Danube frontier, an area that remained under nearly constant siege for many years to come. Prominent among these intruders were the Goths, who would thereafter intermittently play a major role in Roman affairs. According to historian Chris Scarre:

> The Goths, a powerful Germanic people, first appear on the scene as enemies of Rome in the 230s. Later tradition placed their ancestral homeland in southern Sweden, but by the early third century A.D. they had moved south to settle the lands north of the Black Sea. In 238 they crossed the Danube to raid the Balkan provinces of the Roman Empire [Dacia, Moesia], and from 248 they launched a sustained series of attacks, culminating in the defeat and death of the emperor Decius [reigned 249–251] in 251. In 256 and again in 267 they ravaged northwest Asia Minor. . . . Subsequently they split into two parts, the Ostrogoths remaining in the Black Sea region, [and] the Visigoths occupying the abandoned Roman province of Dacia.[31]

While the Goths rampaged, other northern tribes struck deep into imperial territories. In 260, the fierce Alamanni reached Mediolanum (modern Milan), in Italy's Po Valley, where the emperor Gallienus managed, with great difficulty, to stop their southward march. In that same year other tribes devastated large tracts of Gaul, one of the Empire's principal food-growing regions, and some even raided Iberia (Roman Spain). Seven years later, a tribe calling itself the Heruli invaded Greece and sacked Athens, destroying many of the magnificent Greek and Roman buildings for which that cultural center was (and still is) famous.

Meanwhile, the embattled emperors and generals faced attacks on their eastern borders. In the early 240s the newly crowned Sassanian king, Shapur I, began raiding Roman towns; these assaults grew increasingly bold until, in 253 or 254, his forces overran Antioch, in Syria, one of the Empire's largest and most prosperous

The Uppity Queen of Palmyra

This brief account of Zenobia, who dared to challenge Rome, is taken from Vicki León's informative and entertaining book Uppity Women of Ancient Times.

"This politically formidable Arab queen made her home in Palmyra, a fashionable city of 150,000 . . . full of colonnades and fountains, palaces and marble temples, glittering like a strobe-light mirage in the cinnamon-colored Syrian desert. . . . Zenobia claimed descent from one of the early Cleopatras, making her a meld of Macedonian Greek, Arab, and Aramaic blood. Although historians of old had the lazy habit of labeling all famous women as 'beautiful, chaste, and clever,' that may have been an understatement in Zenobia's case. . . . Married at fourteen, she and her king [Odaenath] had just six years together before he was mysteriously killed [possibly by her hand]. . . . Zenobia hungered for power. Her husband was barely cold when she marched into Egypt and took it, then conquered half of Asia Minor for an encore. Only when she declared Palmyran independence from the Empire did Emperor Aurelian of Rome wake up. . . . At the final showdown, he beat Zenobia's forces but it took him two battles to do it. Aurelian gained more than a grudging respect for this fiery queen who could discuss philosophy in three languages. . . . He wanted a proper homecoming triumph, so he forced her to walk through Rome in the traditional parade of prisoners and exotic beasts. . . . (The mind boggles at what parade route conditions must have been like, following the elephants!) Unsinkable even ankle-deep in pachyderm dung, Zenobia finessed a pension for herself instead of the traditional postparade slaughter. To top it off, she talked Aurelian into providing a villa for her and her sons near Tivoli [about thirty miles east of Rome] . . . where she lived in honor for years."

cities, and deported thousands of its inhabitants to Persia. The emperor Valerian, Gallienus's father, led an expedition against the Sassanians in the late 250s, enjoyed some success at first, but then met with disaster in 260. After his army had been decimated by an outbreak of plague and surrounded by Shapur's troops, Valerian made the mistake of agreeing to a face-to-face meeting with the Persian monarch. During the negotiations, Shapur treacherously took the Roman leader and his officers prisoner. For the rest of his life Valerian remained in captivity, forced to crouch down to let Shapur step on his back when mounting his horse.[32]

This 1888 painting titled Zenobia's Last Look on Palmyra *shows her in chains following her capture by the emperor Aurelian.*

Making matters worse for Rome, the failed Sassanian campaign quickly led to a major challenge of a different sort. Odaenath, the local ruler of the thriving trading city of Palmyra, located southeast of Antioch in Syria, at first helped the Romans against Shapur. But then Odaenath suddenly declared himself "King of Kings" of the "Empire" of Palmyra, claiming sovereignty over all of Roman Syria and Palestine. After his death in 267, his widow, the ambitious and formidable Zenobia, invaded and annexed Egypt and parts of Asia Minor. Thus, along with all of its other problems, the Empire faced the potential loss of its eastern provinces, overall its most populous and prosperous region.

Social Pressures and Fading Loyalties

Not surprisingly, the incessant raids, invasions, and civil wars of this period of near anarchy took their toll on everyday Romans. Public works and commerce came to a near standstill, and many areas suffered from periodic bouts of famine and disease epidemics. The German and Persian invaders caused much death and destruction, of course, but equally as bad, if not worse, was the havoc created by Roman soldiers' fighting, robbing, raping, and otherwise abusing their own countrymen. This excerpt from the history penned by a writer of the period, Herodian, probably of Syrian birth, describes how the emperor Maximinus's troops ransacked Aquileia in 238.

Finding the houses of the suburbs deserted [the Aquileians having fled],

Inflation Leads to Corruption

The late and highly respected classical historian A. H. M. Jones offered this appraisal (in Constantine and the Conversion of Europe) *of how inflation—a substantial increase in prices and corresponding decrease in the value of money—affected various sectors of Roman society during the third-century crisis.*

"The vast majority of the inhabitants of the Empire were peasants: those who owned their plots would have profited from the rise in the price of agricultural produce, and the greater number who were tenants would not have suffered, since their rents, being normally fixed by five-year leases, would tend to lag behind prices. . . . As a whole . . . the propertied [landowning] classes would have suffered little, though no doubt some families . . . were ruined. . . . The party most severely hit by the inflation was the government itself, and its salaried and wage-earning servants, more particularly the lower civil servants and the rank and file of the army, who had no other resource than their pay. Taxes brought in only the same nominal amount: the pay therefore of the civil servants and soldiers could not be raised, and they found that it brought them less and less. Soldiers could, and did, help themselves by looting, and civil servants by corruption and extortion: it was during this period that the custom grew up whereby civil servants charged fees to the public for every act they performed—even the tax collector demanded a fee from the taxpayer for the favor of granting a receipt."

they cut down all the vines and trees, set some on fire, and made a shambles of the once-thriving countryside. . . . After destroying all this to the root, the army pressed on to the walls . . . and strove to demolish at least some part of the wall, so that they might break in and sack everything, razing the city and leaving the land a deserted pasturage.[33]

The Empire's general populace experienced a multitude of other problems, combining to make everyday life difficult and uncertain. Although recent scholarship suggests that government taxation of the poorer classes was not as heavy and debilitating as once thought, the effects of forcible confiscation and requirement of service were dire enough. As Starr tells it:

The civil population groaned under the military requisition of food and clothing (called *annona*) and of transport (*angareia*), which at times became simple plundering. The guilds (*collegia*) of shippers were legally bound to the task of supplying Rome with grain; and the *collegia* of butchers and bakers at Rome

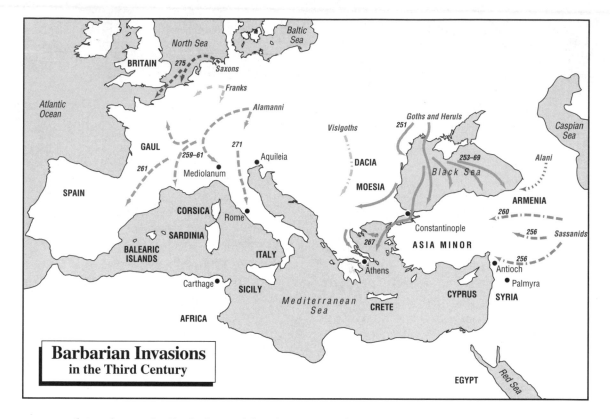

**Barbarian Invasions
in the Third Century**

may have been similarly bound by the reign of Aurelian [ca. 270]. The upper classes of the towns, especially the town councilors (*decurions*), were more and more saddled with compulsory tasks without pay, called *munera* (burdens). Some of these required only service; others involved expenses or the threat of expenses, as in the requirement that the 10 leading councilors see to tax collection and meet any deficiencies out of their own pockets.[34]

Because of these and other social, economic, and military pressures, the traditional order of Roman life steadily and profoundly changed during the third century. The late, great modern Roman scholar A. H. M. Jones offered this discerning assessment:

At one end of the scale peasants began deserting their holdings, either moving to another landlord who offered better terms, or abandoning agriculture altogether for the towns or for a career of banditry. The sons of veterans tended not to enter the army, but preferred to live as gentlemen of leisure on the proceeds of their fathers' discharge gratuities, which usually took the form of land or were invested in land. At the other end of the scale, a large number of senatorial families were killed off or reduced to poverty by the executions and confiscations which often followed a change of emperor. . . . On all sides the old traditions and the old loyalties were fading. . . . The sense of *noblesse oblige* [feelings of duty and obligation to the state and society] was fading among the aristocracy, the spirit of civic patriotism was fast vanishing in the middle class, the discipline of the troops was decaying, and there was nothing to take their place.[35]

Back from the Brink of Doom

By the mid-260s, disunity, chaos, enemy incursions, economic decline, and a deterioration of social order and loyalties appeared to spell the end of the old Roman world. However, the same resiliency and spirit of determination that had pulled Rome back from the brink of doom on many occasions in its long history now once more came to the fore. Beginning in 268, a series of strong military leaders took control and, as Michael Grant terms it, "in one of the most striking reversals in world history, Rome's foes were hurled back."[36]

First, the emperor Claudius II inflicted a crushing defeat on the Alamanni in the autumn of 268; in the following year he campaigned successfully against the Goths, an effort that won him the title of "Gothicus." Aurelian (reigned 270–275), who bore the nickname "Hand on Hilt," also defeated the Alamanni, along with a newly arrived tribe, the Vandals. In addition, he built a defensive wall around the imperial capital twelve miles in circumference, twelve feet thick, and twenty feet high; defeated the Goths in a series of engagements along the Danube frontier; and in 273 captured Palmyra, dismantling Zenobia's short-lived realm and afterward settling her in a villa near Rome.[37] Probus and Carus, two of Aurelian's successors, also distinguished themselves in defeating the Empire's enemies and helping to restore its unity.

The shrewdest, most talented, and by far most successful of this group of strong military emperors emerged in 284. When the young emperor Numerian was murdered by one of his own officers, Arrius Aper, while leading his army home from a campaign against the Sassanians, the soldiers selected the head of the household cavalry, one Diocles, to carry out the punishment. Diocles did so in a bold way, stabbing Aper to death in full view of the assembled troops. They then proceeded to proclaim him emperor, after which he changed his name to Diocletian. Under his guidance, the Empire would continue its recovery from the century of crisis and enjoy a fresh start, although this new Rome, what we now call the Later Empire, would be a harsher, graver, less hopeful place than the Empire of the *Pax Romana*. The inhabitants of the earlier, still prosperous realm believed in their hearts that Rome was invincible; those of the Later Empire, having barely escaped utter collapse and annihilation, knew otherwise.

Chapter

3 Order and Security Restored: Diocletian Reorganizes the Empire

On his accession to the Roman imperial throne on November 20, 284, Diocletian was about thirty-nine years old. He hailed from the town of Spalato (or Split), on the coast of Dalmatia, lying directly across the narrow Adriatic Sea from eastern Italy. Of humble origins, his father having been a scribe (or, as some sources claim, the freed slave of a wealthy senator), he enlisted in the army as a young man and, through a combination of talent and hard work, rose steadily through the ranks. For all anyone knew on that November day when he assumed power over the Roman realm, he might prove to be just another in a long line of gruff and grasping soldier-emperors; considering the course of recent history, the odds were that he would die by assassination after a short and at best moderately productive reign.

However, Diocletian defied and beat the odds. He ruled for more than twenty years, the longest imperial reign since that of the fourth "good" emperor, Antoninus Pius (ruled 138–161), and vacated the throne voluntarily, an act unprecedented in the Empire's history. More important, those twenty-odd years were packed with productivity. While restoring relative peace and unity to Rome, Diocletian substantially reorganized the provinces, the tax system, the imperial administration and court, and the army, initiating what was in effect a new Roman Empire.

Most of Diocletian's sweeping reforms were maintained or expanded by his successors, most notably Constantine I, who

This bust, now in the Capitoline Museum in Rome, depicts Diocletian, who completely reorganized the Empire in the late third century.

became emperor in 307, two years after Diocletian's retirement, and ruled for thirty years. In most domestic affairs, Constantine was Diocletian's heir (they differed mainly on religion); as Averil Cameron puts it, "many of the social, administrative, and economic developments in his [Constantine's] reign simply brought Diocletian's innovations to their logical conclusion."[38] Although Diocletian, as the initial innovator, must be accorded the lion's share of the credit, their reforms are best examined together, as an ongoing process. During their combined reigns, they infused what had appeared to be a doomed realm with more than another century of vigorous life and made it possible for Rome to pass on much of its rich cultural legacy to later ages.

Rome's New Court and Provinces

On becoming emperor, Diocletian determined that he would not, as so many of his immediate predecessors had, be struck down in his prime before accomplishing anything constructive or lasting. To help protect himself from assassination and at the same time restore the imperial throne's sagging prestige and authority, he fashioned the Roman court into an "eastern"-style absolute monarchy, using Sassanian Persia as a model. He began wearing sumptuous silk robes embroidered with gold and studded with precious gems. And he made himself aloof and secluded from all but a privileged few. Gone now was any pretense about Rome's emperor being a man of the people, the *princeps,* or first citizen, as Augustus and his successors had

called themselves. Instead, Diocletian called himself *dominus,* or lord, allowed people to address him as "adored one," demanded that those who approached him bow low and kiss his hand or robe, and filled the Roman court with elaborate ceremony, ordering, for example, that trumpets be sounded when he entered. Constantine later carried on this tradition. A panel on his famous arch (which stands near the Colosseum) shows him granting an audience to petitioners half his size who huddle gazing up at his superhuman form. These and other similar measures had the desired effect of surrounding the throne with an air of awe and superstition that made would-be assassins think twice.[39]

The newly remodeled Roman court and imperial household required a huge supporting staff. A. H. M. Jones lists some of the emperor's retinue, most of whom followed him wherever he traveled:

The inner sanctum of the "sacred bedchamber" was attended by a corps of eunuchs [castrated males], who, despite their servile birth and barbarian origins, were persons of some political consequence, since they controlled access to the emperor. The emperor's person was guarded by a corps of officer cadets, selected from the ranks of the army and destined after service on the staff to be promoted tribunes [officers] of units. Closely attached to the emperor were the secretariats, under the control of the Master of the Sacred Memory, apparently a private secretary; the Master of Studies, who seems to have controlled the registries and archives; the Masters of Latin and Greek Letters, who drafted outgoing correspondences in the two languages, and the Master of Petitions, who prepared [answers] to complaints and requests from subjects. The personnel of the secretariats was controlled by . . . the Tribune and Master of the Offices, who also had charge of the offices which arranged audiences with the emperor and organized his itinerary, and a body of interpreters to deal with foreign envoys.[40]

Members of this retinue, along with their thousands of "inspectors," who were stationed around the Empire and reported back to the Master of the Offices, were hated and feared by the public. It was, ironically, no secret that these officials acted as the "secret police" who helped the emperor maintain his autocratic power.

Diocletian's new bureaucracy extended outward from the central administration to the Empire's far-flung provinces. Many of these were large and populous, which not only made them difficult to administer but also provided ample recruits and supplies to ambitious governors with an eye to challenging the throne. Under Diocletian's reforms, Cameron explains,

> military and civil commands were separated and each province henceforth had both a military commander [the *dux,* or duke] and a civil governor. The provinces themselves were reduced in size and greatly enlarged in number [from about fifty to one hundred]. . . . The aim was to secure greater efficiency by shortening the chain of communications and command, and in so doing to reduce the power of individual governors.[41]

To help relieve the central government of the massive increase in administrative duties accompanying the new plan, Diocletian created a new governmental unit between the center and the provinces—the diocese. He grouped the provinces into thirteen regional dioceses, each administered by a *vicarius,* or vicar. In this new three-tiered system, the governors reported to the vicars, who reported to three (later four) top imperial ministers, the praetorian prefects, who, in their turn, reported to the emperor.

The Formation of the Tetrarchy

Despite these administrative reforms, Diocletian realized that ruling so vast a realm was still too difficult for one man, so he shrewdly delegated power to a trusted few. In March 286, he appointed Maximian, another soldier of humble birth who had risen through the ranks, as "Caesar," second in command and heir to the throne; at the same time the older man formally adopted the younger as his son. About six months later, Diocletian went a step further and bestowed on Maximian the title of Augustus, making him in effect a co-emperor. The senior Augustus, Diocletian, hereafter ruled from the city of Nicomedia in northern Asia Minor, while the other took charge of the western part of the realm.

Later, in 293, Diocletian divided imperial power still further, both he and Maximian appointing Caesars of their own—the prominent army leaders Galerius and Constantius. As the proud symbol of the Empire's new order, this four-man combination, known as the Tetrarchy, was celebrated in glowing propaganda on coins, monuments, and in panegyrics like the one recorded in the *Augustan History:* "Four rulers of the world they were indeed, brave, wise, kind, generous, respectful to the Senate, friends of the people, moderate, revered, devoted, pious."[42] A more realistic appraisal came from the fourth-century Roman historian Aurelius Victor:

> All these men were, indeed, natives of Illyria [the region that became Yugoslavia in modern times]; but although little cultured, they were of great service to the state, because they were inured [accustomed] to the hardships of rural life and of war. . . . The harmony which prevailed among them proved above all that their native ability and their skill in military science, which they had acquired from [the strong soldier-emperors] Aurelian and Probus, almost sufficed to compensate for lack of high character.[43]

It must be emphasized that the tetrarchs were not equal partners in power. Diocletian remained the senior member, dominating and controlling the others, although Victor's assertion that the other three "looked up to Diocletian as to a father or as one would to a mighty god"[44] is undoubtedly an exaggeration. The senior Augustus knew full well that their unity, resting mainly on mutual consent, was fragile, so he took some precautionary measures, among them keeping Constantius's son, Constantine, then about nineteen or twenty, in Nicomedia as insurance for his father's good behavior in the west. This turned out to be unnecessary, as Constantius proved a loyal and effective ruler. He crossed over into Britain and defeated a usurper, Allectus;[45] restored the ruined cities of the region; and beat back several German incursions into the frontier of the Rhine River, the eastern border of Rome's fertile Gallic provinces.

One significant consequence of all this redistribution of administrative and military power was that the importance and status of the city of Rome, long the grand capital and hub of the Empire and known world, greatly diminished. As Professor Jones correctly observed,

> Rome was already in Diocletian's day an anachronism. It had ceased to be the capital of the Empire in any but a formal

This famous sculpture, now on display at St. Mark's Church in Venice, depicts the tetrarchs, Diocletian, Maximian, Galerius, and Constantius, symbolically embracing one another.

sense, and it never became so again. As an administrative center, Rome was under the Later Empire of no greater importance than a dozen other cities which were capitals of dioceses.[46]

Among these newer regional capitals were, in addition to Nicomedia, Diocletian's main residence, Serdica (Sofia) and Sirmium, both situated in strategic positions not far south of the Danube frontier; Thessalonica, in northern Greece; and Augusta Treviorum (Trier), west of the Rhine in northern Gaul. Other cities that became prominent in this period, partly because

The Tetrarchs Bound by Marriage and Adoption

In this excerpt from Constantine and Eusebius, *historian Timothy Barnes explains how Diocletian and his fellow tetrarchs further cemented their grand alliance through the use of the traditional, respectable social ties, particularly marriage and adoption. This process also assured that Constantine would be a strong contender in the future imperial succession.*

"The Roman Empire was in theory an elective monarchy: the Senate or the preceding emperor would appoint a new emperor solely on the basis of his fitness to rule. In practice, however, succession was always hereditary: no emperor whose rule was secure had ever excluded his sons from the succession, and emperors who appointed heirs not of their blood customarily adopted them in a formal ceremony. In 293, therefore, Diocletian and Maximian, who, as Augusti, styled themselves brothers, adopted Galerius and Constantius as their sons. The Augusti and the Caesars were also linked by marriage: Constantius had married Theodora, the daughter of Maximian, at least as early as 289, and it must be suspected that Galerius's marriage to Valeria, the daughter of Diocletian, also antedates his elevation to the purple. These alliances by marriage did more than combine the four reigning emperors to one another. They advertised to the world the identity of their prospective heirs. . . . Diocletian may have summoned Maxentius [Maximian's young son] to his court to groom him for the throne. The adult son of Constantius was the other obvious candidate for the imperial succession. Constantine was soon summoned to Diocletian's court, and a mosaic in the banquet room of the imperial palace at Aquileia depicted his departure from the West in a scene with Fausta, the young daughter of Maximian, offering him a plumed helmet which gleamed with gold and precious jewels."

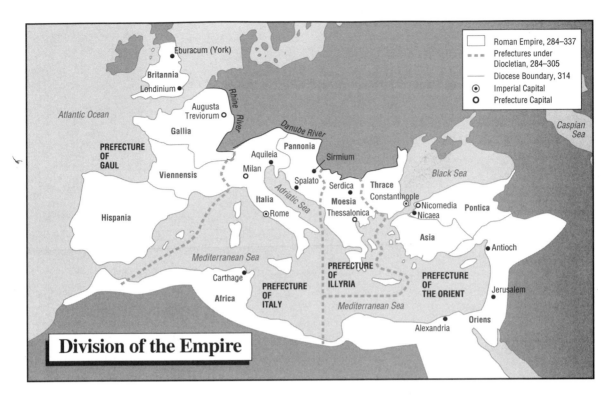

Division of the Empire

the emperors visited them often, were Milan and Aquileia, both in northern Italy, and Naissus (Nis), near Serdica.

Military Reforms

One of Diocletian's most important reform efforts, one that Constantine later developed more fully, was an overhaul of the Roman military. The army's new composition reflected a general change in the Empire's overall defensive strategy that had been developing for some time. This strategy, growing out of the realities of more than a century of nearly relentless barbarian incursions in the north, was based on the assumption that it was no longer possible to make the borders, or *limes,* completely impregnable; some in-

vaders must be expected to get through the line of forts on the frontier. However, these intruders could be intercepted by one or more small, swiftly moving mobile armies stationed at key points in the border provinces. To make such "defense-in-depth" strategy work, historian Arther Ferrill points out, "the forts must be strong enough to withstand attack and yet not so strongly defended as to become a drain on manpower weakening the mobile army."[47]

The emperor Gallienus had taken a step in this direction of less static defenses in the 260s by recruiting extra cavalry forces for a mobile army that could move independently of the slow-moving main legions. Diocletian now took the idea a step further. He stationed small armies, each accompanied by detachments of cavalry, called *vexillationes,* at key positions on the frontiers. He also attached two highly

An Ancient Critique of Constantine's Military Policy

Zosimus was a fifth-century Greek historian whose Recent History *covers Diocletian's and Constantine's reigns. This excerpt, quoted in Lewis and Reinhold's* Sourcebook 2, *criticizes Constantine for weakening the frontier military garrisons.*

"Constantine likewise took another measure, which gave the barbarians unhindered access into the lands subject to the Romans. For the Roman Empire was, by the foresight of Diocletian, everywhere protected on its frontiers . . . by towns and fortresses and towers, in which the entire army was stationed; it was thus impossible for the barbarians to cross over, there being everywhere a sufficient opposing force to repel their inroads. But Constantine destroyed that security by removing the greater part of the soldiers from the frontiers and stationing them in cities that did not require protection; thus he stripped those of protection who were harassed by the barbarians and brought ruin to peaceful cities at the hands of the soldiers by exposing them to shows and luxuries. To speak plainly, he was the first to sow the seeds of the ruinous state of affairs that has lasted up to the present time."

trained legions to his personal traveling court, the *comitatus,* supported by elite cavalry forces, the *scholae,* thus creating a fast and very effective mobile field force. Classical scholars Lesley and Roy Adkins explain how Constantine later expanded this approach:

> Constantine I also divided the army into mobile forces (*comitatenses*—from *comitatus*) and frontier troops (*limitanei*—from *limes*). Constantine withdrew troops from many frontier positions and instead concentrated mobile forces at key points in the frontier zone in order to react to any local incursions, while the remaining army was posted in garrisons. The *comitatenses* did not have fixed garrisons,

but were either on campaign or were stationed in towns. They were used for attacking opponents in the field.[48]

The actual size of these armies, as well as of Rome's overall forces, is difficult to calculate and often disputed. A realistic figure for the Empire's combined armies in the first half of the fourth century is perhaps four hundred thousand. At first glance this sounds truly formidable. But we must factor into it realities such as the inflation of army lists with fictitious entries (names of little boys and old men inserted in attempts to draw their pay and rations); high desertion rates, spotty training, and inadequate supplies (caused in large part because of the government's shortage of funds); and the fact that these forces were dispersed across a huge realm. Individual field armies were very small in comparison to those of republican times. Each of Constantine's mobile army units likely consisted of little more than one thousand infantry and five hundred cavalry. These were often combined to form larger armies, of course, but only rarely did generals in the Later Empire field forces numbering in the tens of thousands.[49]

Even these smaller armies were not easy to raise and maintain. Thanks to the horrors of the third-century crisis, fewer Roman men enlisted in the army than had in prior, more peaceful times. So to keep troop numbers up, Diocletian made service for the sons of veterans compulsory. Historian Stewart Perowne describes some of the reasons why conscription remained unpopular and difficult to enforce:

Those who tried to evade their duty were liable to be rounded up by recruiting officers. Every estate or village, or group of villages, had to provide so many recruits every so

Roman troops of the Later Empire clash with Germans near one of the northern frontiers. These frontiers were guarded by a chain of forts, but some invaders still got through.

many years. The levy fell wholly on the rural population. The age-limits were from nineteen to thirty-five, and the height qualification was five foot ten, reduced later to five foot seven. As soon as they were enrolled, recruits were branded, as a precaution against desertion. This fact alone shows how unpopular the service had become, and consequently how hard it now was to find enough recruits.[50]

Thus, despite Diocletian's and Constantine's military reforms, which helped maintain the Later Empire's newfound sense of order and safety, increasing numbers of Roman men avoided military service. Over time this ominous trend would have serious consequences for the realm.

Overhauling the Economy

Not surprisingly, the new imperial order, with its swollen ranks of salaried civil servants and soldiers, was extremely expensive to maintain. And high inflation and nearly worthless money, two of the crippling by-products of the chaotic third century, still plagued Roman society. So Diocletian instituted large-scale measures to overhaul the Empire's economy. His first move, instituted in the 290s, was an attempt to stabilize the money supply by issuing pure gold and silver coins. This failed, apparently because his supplies of these precious metals were limited. He had to continue to pay the troops and many others with devalued coins, which kept inflation high. Constantine later tried a similar tactic, issuing a gold coin called the *solidus,* which, although it remained in circulation

well into the Middle Ages, did not succeed in stopping inflation in his own time.

Taking a different approach, Diocletian next tried to regulate prices and wages, believing that such an effort would keep inflation down and the economy stable. The introduction to his famous economic edict, issued in 301, stated in part:

> With mankind itself now appearing to be praying for release [from economic misery], we have decreed that there be established . . . a maximum [ceiling for prices and wages], so that when the violence of high prices appears anywhere—may the gods avert such a calamity! . . . It is our pleasure . . . that the prices listed in the subjoined [attached] summary be observed in the whole of our empire.[51]

Among the prices listed in the summary: A six-hundred-pound camel-load could not cost more than eight *denarii* a mile to transport, a pair of women's boots could cost no more than sixty *denarii*, and a carpenter could charge up to, but not more than, fifty *denarii* a day. Though well-meaning, this approach failed too, primarily because people resented being told what they could earn or charge for goods, and they either ignored or found ways to subvert the edict. The Christian writer Lactantius recorded the policy's demise in this overdramatic but not wholly inaccurate critique: "Much blood was shed on paltry and trifling charges, and nothing appeared on the market for fear, until, inevitably, after many had died, the law was relaxed."[52]

While his efforts to stabilize the currency and regulate prices proved short-lived, two other socioeconomic policies

Diocletian's Edict on Prices

These are excerpts from the opening section of Diocletian's famous economic edict of 301 (quoted in Paul Alexander's The Ancient World*), in which he attempted (ultimately in vain) to stabilize the Roman economy by setting maximum prices that people could charge for goods and services.*

"We, who by the gracious favor of the gods have repressed the former tide of ravages of barbarian nations by destroying them, must guard by the due defenses of justice a peace which was established for eternity. If, indeed, any self-restraint might check the excesses with which limitless and furious avarice [greed] rages . . . there would perhaps be some room for . . . silence [inaction]. . . . Since, however, it is the sole desire of unrestrained madness to have no thought for the common need . . . we—the protectors of the human race—viewing the situation, have agreed that justice should intervene . . . so that the long-hoped-for solution which mankind itself could not supply might . . . be applied to the general betterment of all. . . . We, therefore, hasten to apply the remedies long demanded by the [crippling economic] situation, satisfied that there can be no complaints. . . . Aroused justly and rightfully by all the facts which are detailed above, and with mankind itself now appearing to be praying for release [from economic misery], we have decreed that there be established . . . a maximum [ceiling for prices and wages], so that when the violence of high prices appears anywhere—may the gods avert such a calamity! . . . It is our pleasure . . . that the prices listed in the subjoined [attached] summary be observed in the whole of our empire. We . . . urge upon the loyalty of all our people that a law constituted for the public good may be observed with willing obedience and due care."

Diocletian instituted had long-lasting consequences. Because money was worth so little, Roman tax collectors had long accepted goods such as livestock, jewelry, and food as payment. By the early fourth century, this payment in kind, or indiction (from the Latin *indictiones),* formed the bulk of government revenue. But it was levied in a haphazard and inequitable fashion, and the state, having no idea how much it would collect in a given year, was unable to plan ahead. So Diocletian ordered a series of regional censuses (which were not completed until after his abdication) designed to assess the worth of land, livestock, and other property throughout

Roman pistores, *miller-bakers, seen in this restoration of a bakery found in the ruins of Pompeii, were among the many workers ordered to remain in their professions for life.*

the Empire. Under his immediate successors, including Constantine, these assessments formed the basis of fairer tax payments from individuals; they also helped government planners, who now had at least a rough idea of how much the state could expect to collect each year.

Another of Diocletian's policies had even more long-lasting, but also more ominous and repressive, effects. To make sure that goods and services continued uninterrupted, he and his successors ordered that nearly all workers remain in their present profession for life. "If any shipmaster by birth becomes captain of a lighter [a barge for loading and unloading ships]," stated one such law, "he shall . . . continue right along to remain in the same group in which his parents appear to have been."[53] Similar legislation steadily transformed the *coloni,* poor tenant farmers bound in service to wealthy landlords, into hapless and hopeless "slaves of the soil." A law passed under Constantine declared:

Any person whatsoever in whose possession a [runaway] *colonus* belonging to another is found not only shall restore the said *colonus* to his place of origin but shall also assume the capitation [poll or head] tax on him for the time [that he had him]. And as for *coloni* themselves, it will be proper for such as contemplate flight to be bound with chains to a servile status, so that by virtue of such condemnation to servitude they may be compelled to fulfill the duties that benefit free men.[54]

Another group that suffered heavily from such laws was town officials, the *decurions,* whose financial burdens (including meeting tax shortfalls from their own pockets) had already become unfair and oppressive before Diocletian's time. Increasingly locked into their own hell of hereditary servitude in the fourth century, many of these officials tried to evade their duties by entering the army or the clergy.[55]

Rome's Rebirth an Illusion

Thus, most of the reforms initiated by Diocletian and carried on by his successors were far reaching, affecting the lives of Romans of all classes over several generations. Thanks to these efforts, the Later Empire benefited from a restoration of much of the order and security lost in the turbulent third century; however, these benefits came at the price of a more regimented, creatively stifled, and despondent populace. Most people went along with the new order simply because they felt they had no other choice. The emperors had their armies of spies and soldiers to enforce their decrees, after all.

In the long run, this seeming recovery and rebirth of the Roman Empire would prove illusory and temporary. Evident now, but unbeknownst to the emperors and their subjects then, the underpinnings of their realm were inherently weak; and collapse was, sooner or later, more or less inevitable. In the final analysis, though Rome was one of the greatest civilizations of ancient times, by modern economic and technological standards it was very backward. Professor Jones gave this penetrating analysis:

> There were coming to be more idle mouths than the primitive economic system of the Roman Empire could feed. It is hard to remember that, despite its great achievements in law and administration, the splendid architecture of its cities and the luxurious standard of living of its aristocracy, the Roman Empire was, in its methods of production, in some ways more primitive than the early Middle Ages. Agriculture followed a wasteful two-field system of alternate crop and fallow. Yarn was spun by hand with a spindle, and textiles laboriously woven on clumsy hand looms. Even corn was ground in hand querns or at best mills turned by oxen: windmills had not been invented and watermills were still rare. In these circumstances the feeding and clothing of an individual demanded a vast expenditure of human labor, and the maintenance of any substantial number of economically unproductive persons laid a heavy burden on the rest.[56]

In spite of Diocletian's and Constantine's reforms, therefore, Rome continued to undergo a slow and subtle economic decline, the most dire effects of which would not be felt until the next century.

4 "Conquer by This": Constantine and the Triumph of Christianity

Although Constantine maintained and expanded on many of the political and military policies initiated by Diocletian and the Tetrarchy, he is best known for championing the Christians. During Constantine's reign, Christianity underwent a relatively sudden transition from a minor, misunderstood, often hated, and persecuted faith, to a widely tolerated, legally sanctioned, and rapidly growing one.

Thanks in large degree to Constantine's pro-Christian policies, only a few decades after his death the faith became the Empire's official religion.

The reasons Christianity was able to make such phenomenal gains in so short a time are not hard to fathom. Mostly as a result of the terrors of the century of crisis, the Roman populace had undergone a significant change of attitude. The old opti-

A Christian funeral procession passes a group of Roman revelers on the Appian Way, one of Italy's main roads, sometime in the first century A.D.

mistic belief that Rome had been chosen by the gods to rule the world forever had been steadily replaced by feelings of hopelessness, despair, and apathy. Some felt that the gods they worshiped had abandoned them and, searching for comfort, they embraced other gods, among these the Christian one. One aspect of Christianity that appealed to many, especially the poor and downtrodden, was its promise that everyone, from the loftiest king to the lowliest slave, could find happiness in life after death. According to classical scholar L. P. Wilkinson, the Christians

> brought to ordinary people of both sexes, often slaves, a simple and joyful message of love and hope that was not so novel as to be unacceptable or incomprehensible . . . hope of an eternity of bliss for believers as a compensation for the trials of this life. Their community was a haven for the lonely. . . . The Christians' exclusiveness also preserved them. . . . They refused to compromise . . . or indeed to see any value in any other religion. . . . Finally, they prospered just because they were persecuted. . . . Their suffering drew them together for comfort and in loyalty. Besides . . . in bitter times men turn with much more alacrity [quickness] to religion.[57]

Indeed, the anxious, economically disastrous times of the mid–third century, during which the Empire neared collapse, probably benefited Christianity by swelling its ranks with fearful, hopeless, desperate people.

In spite of these factors, however, Christianity would not have spread so quickly, and perhaps would never have triumphed at all, had it not been for Constantine. His granting its members toleration and economic and other privileges, his construction of churches and of Constantinople, the first truly Christian city, and his eventual conversion to the faith were key factors in its gaining social acceptance and new converts. Considering Christianity's profound influence on Rome in its final years, as well as on succeeding ages, Constantine's thirty-year reign undoubtedly marks one of the major turning points in European history.

Maxentius, the Miracles, and the Milvian Bridge

Constantine's first important dealings with Christianity were part of the dramatic series of events that elevated him to ultimate power over the Roman realm. When Diocletian retired in 305 (to a palace in his native town of Spalato), he ordered Maximian, still the Augustus of the Empire's western half, to step down also. The plan was for the two Caesars, Galerius and Constantius, to become the Augusti of a new tetrarchy. And to that end, Diocletian chose another veteran army general, Severus, as Constantius's Caesar and Maximin (or Maximinus Daia), Galerius's young nephew, as Caesar to Galerius.

Diocletian hoped that the succession and subsequent rule of these men would prove orderly and productive. But he was soon bitterly disappointed. In the next few years, a power struggle among Maximian, Galerius, Constantius, and some of their sons developed into a full-fledged civil war in which several different men proclaimed themselves emperor (or were proclaimed by their troops) while fighting major battles all over the Empire. Among these

A nineteenth-century rendering of the miraculous celestial vision supposedly witnessed by Constantine and his men as they approached Rome to unseat the usurper, Maxentius.

strange insignia—what looked like the letter *X* superimposed over a letter *P*.

Maxentius did not realize that this was a Christian symbol, composed of chi and rho, the first two letters of Christos, the Greek version of Christ's name. According to Constantine's contemporary biographer, the Christian bishop Eusebius, the emperor later told him that the day before,

> [at] about noon, when the day was already beginning to decline, he saw with his own eyes the trophy of a cross of light in the heavens, above the sun, and an inscription, "CONQUER BY THIS," attached to it. At this sight he himself was struck with amazement, and his whole army also, which . . . witnessed the miracle. . . . And while he continued to ponder and reason on its meaning, night overtook him; then in his sleep the Christ of God appeared to him . . . and commanded him to make a likeness of that sign which he had seen in the heavens, and to use it as a safeguard in all engagements with his enemies.[59]

Over the ages, arguments have raged about what Constantine and his men actually saw in the sky, whether it was indeed a miracle, or perhaps a delusion or misidentification of some natural phenomenon. Most modern scholars agree with A. H. M. Jones's assessment that it was a solar halo, caused by the fall of "ice crystals across the rays of the sun. It usually takes the form of mock suns or of rings of light surrounding the sun, but a cross of light with the sun in its center has been on several occasions scientifically observed. The display may well have been brief . . . but to Constantine's overwrought imagination it was deeply significant."[60] According to this view, the

claimants was Constantine, named Augustus at his father's unexpected death in 306.[58] Many Romans worried that the realm might be slipping back into the near anarchy of the third century.

But these new civil discords were thankfully relatively short-lived. Their climax came in 312, when Constantine marched his army into Italy with the goal of unseating Maxentius, Maximian's son, who had illegally declared himself emperor and seized the city of Rome. Hoping to intercept and destroy the approaching enemy, Maxentius led his own troops out of the city via the Milvian Bridge and onto the Flaminian Way, the road running north along the Tiber. Soon he found the route blocked by Constantine's soldiers, whose shields bore a words "Conquer by This" and the subsequent dream were added later by Eusebius to strengthen the connection between Christ and Constantine and thereby to help empower the faith.

Whatever Constantine's motivation for adopting a Christian symbol may have been, there can be little doubt that he believed its power won the day for him. Maxentius retreated back to the Milvian Bridge, where the two armies clashed, a bloodbath ensued, and he and several thousand of his men drowned in the Tiber. The next day, October 29, 312, Constantine entered Rome in triumph. Proudly displayed on his helmet was the chi-rho sign, which he used as his battle token ever after.

Christianity in the Religious Melting Pot

Constantine's sighting of the unexpected sign in the sky and subsequent victory seem to satisfactorily explain the favor and support he showed the Christians thereafter. Like nearly all other people of his day, he was both deeply religious and highly superstitious.[61] And he could be expected not only to attribute his win to the Christian god, but also to handsomely repay that deity by helping its followers. It must be emphasized that Constantine did not actually convert to the faith at this moment. For a long time he remained a pagan, or non-Christian, who accepted the existence of and showed favor and gratitude to the Christian god. At first this must have perplexed many of his pagan subjects, for the Christians were at the time still few in number (2 to 10 percent of the population at most) and generally detested.

A brief examination of how Christianity differed from and competed with other beliefs current at that time sheds some light on how Constantine's subjects viewed it and why he championed it. In their first three centuries, the Christians' tiny ranks grew very slowly, partly because their beliefs were vastly overshadowed by the wide array of popular faiths practiced in the Empire. Prominent were the traditional major gods, including Jupiter, Juno, Mars, Minerva, and Apollo, making up the sacred pantheon of the official state religion. The Romans also worshiped many very ancient personal and household spirits, among them the *lares,* who were thought to keep the house safe, and the *manes,* spirits of deceased ancestors.

Particularly popular in Rome's religious melting pot were several eastern "mystery" cults imported into Italy and the western provinces during late republican times. The oldest and most widely accepted of these was that of Cybele, the "Great Mother," from Asia Minor, a nature and fertility goddess whose priests castrated themselves to appease her. Her striking initiation rite involved placing the candidate in a pit under a grid; on the grid the priests sacrificed a bull, allowing its blood to flow down on the person, who was thereby "reborn" as a member of the faith. Other important mystery cults centered around Isis, an Egyptian deity whom the Romans associated with goodness and purification of sin, and Mithras, from Persia, whose followers preached treating all people with kindness and respect.

Christianity, itself an eastern cult (its birthplace being Palestine), had many elements in common with the others. Like Mithraism, for example, it featured the miraculous birth of a sacred baby, a sacramental meal of bread and water (or wine), baptism, and the promise of resurrection. Also, explains Charles Freeman:

> Much of the imagery of the New Testament—light and darkness, faith compared to flourishing crops—is similar to that found in mystery religions. . . . The development of the cult of Mary, the mother of Jesus, acquires a new richness when placed in parallel with the worship of other mother figures in these religions. . . . Many of the procedures of the mystery religions (initiation into the cult, for instance) were to act as important influences on Christian practice.[62]

A natural question is why did Christianity, sharing so many features with other widely popular faiths, remain so *un*popular until Constantine's time? After all, the Romans were uniquely generous in their religious tolerance, as evidenced by the Empire's broad proliferation of gods and beliefs. Out of a sense of patriotism and shared tradition, people of all faiths paid at least occasional homage to the state gods and also to the emperor, whom for political reasons the state represented as semidivine. And members of one faith almost always showed respect for the gods of other faiths. Indeed, belief in syncretism, the idea that all human gods are varied conceptions of one all-powerful god, was common. To an average Roman, worshiping a certain preferred god or gods did not suggest that all other gods were false or inferior; most people matter-of-factly accepted the notion that there were many diverse paths to the same heavenly truths.

Yet for generations, most Romans viewed the Christians with suspicion, hatred, and even disgust. Respected scholar Harold Mattingly lists some of what were, given the circumstances at the time, quite understandable reasons:

The followers of Cybele, a fertility goddess also known as Magna Mater, *the Great Mother, believed that she was the mother of all living things and that she could both cause and cure disease.*

> They [the Christians] refused to worship the [state] gods, insisting on the supremacy of one god of their own; at the same time they paid extraordinary honor to their founder, who had actually been crucified as a dangerous agitator by the Roman governor of Judea. They were inclined to abstain from the good things of life—from theaters, banquets, shows of amphitheater and circus. More than this, they were suspected of horrible crimes—child murder, incest . . . suspicions that perhaps arose out of genuine misunderstanding of . . . Christian [rituals].[63]

The Last Persecution

In this excerpt from The Deaths of the Persecutors, *the Christian writer Lactantius describes episodes from the last and worst Christian persecution, ordered in 303 by Diocletian and Galerius.*

"Suddenly, while it was still not full daylight, the prefect came to the church with . . . tribunes and officers of the treasury. They tore down the door and searched for a picture or image of God. When the Scriptures were found, they were burned. The chance for booty was given to all. . . . The next day the edict was published in which it was ordered that men of that religion should be deprived of all honor and dignity and be subjected to torments. . . . It was with great courage that a certain man pulled down and tore up this edict. . . . Immediately, he was taken, and he was not only tortured, but he was actually cooked . . . and then finally burned up, having suffered with admirable patience."

For these reasons, over time the Christians acquired the terrible stigma of having *odium generis humani,* a "hatred for the human race."[64] Worst of all, at least from the state's viewpoint, they would not take part in emperor worship, a refusal viewed by Roman officials as a potential threat to public order. Since the Christians were an antisocial, criminal element that posed a threat to society, went the conventional reasoning, they needed to be restrained and punished before they seriously harmed the community. This was, more or less, the rationale for the series of persecutions the Roman government carried out against them in the first three centuries A.D.

Constantine himself witnessed the worst of these persecutions, which began in the closing years of Diocletian's reign. The chief tetrarch had long tolerated the Christians, although somewhat reluctantly. A conservative, old-fashioned man, he did not favor the more popular gods of the day, such as Mithras and Cybele, preferring to worship Jupiter, the traditional patron deity of the Roman state. Fables about the Christians committing incest in their secret rites still persisted, and Diocletian often worried that such acts might anger the traditional gods and turn them against Rome. Nevertheless, he took no overt action against the Christians until early in 303. During a customary state sacrifice that year, the priests reported that the livers of the slaughtered animals showed no markings, an unusual occurrence; when the concerned emperor asked why, they claimed that some Christians among the imperial retinue had hexed the ceremony by making the magical sign of the cross.

Furious, Diocletian at first ordered that all Christians in the army and civil service be expelled unless they made public sacrifice to the traditional gods. But his Caesar,

Galerius, a vehement anti-Christian, argued that this action was too lenient. At Galerius's instigation, on February 23, 303, the government posted an edict ordering the closing of all Christian churches, the surrender and burning of the Scriptures, and the banning of Christian religious meetings. Other edicts followed and along with them much bloodshed and misery, mainly in the east under the fanatical Galerius, joined later by his nephew Maximin. Eusebius recounted some of the horrors:

> We saw with our very eyes the houses of prayer cast down to their foundations . . . and the inspired and sacred Scriptures committed to the flames in the midst of the marketplaces. . . . The spectacle of what followed surpasses all description; for in every place a countless number were shut up, and everywhere the prisons, that long ago had been prepared for murderers and grave robbers, were then filled with [Christians] . . . so that there was no longer any room left for [real criminals].[65]

The Unconquered Sun

By contrast, in much of the western part of the realm, where Maximian and Constantius held sway, Christians largely escaped persecution. To his credit, Maximian apparently did not post the later anti-Christian edicts; Constantius, in charge of Britain and Gaul, closed the churches but took no further action. When Constantine succeeded his father in 306, he pursued an even more humane policy, granting the Christians in the provinces he controlled complete toleration.

Constantine, seen in this likeness from a gold coin now in the British Museum, pursued a humane policy toward the Christians of Gaul and Britain, granting them complete toleration. Later, he did the same for Christians all over the Empire.

Thus, it appears that by the time of the battle at the Milvian Bridge, six years later, Constantine was already on good terms with the Christians. This partly explains why he so readily adopted their symbol and called on their god to help him attain victory. Viewing Christianity as a legitimate religion, one as worthy as any other practiced in the Empire, in typical Roman fashion he accorded it the same respect as the others, including, of course, acceptance of the existence of the Christian god.

Furthermore, because of the spectacular solar halo he had seen in the sky, he now associated that deity with the one he had for some time worshiped—the Unconquered Sun. Another eastern religious import, the Sun had become increasingly popular in the third century; Septimius

Severus's wife had become a devotee; the emperor Aurelian had established an elaborate temple for the god, complete with a priesthood, in Rome in 274; and during Diocletian's reign the faith grew rapidly, attracting many Roman notables, including Constantine. On the day before the battle, then, religious syncretism must have come to the fore. In Constantine's hour of need, Professor Jones suggested,

> the Sun had sent him a sign; and that sign was the Cross, the symbol of the Christians. Whatever this signified, that Christ was a manifestation of the Unconquered Sun, or that the Sun was the symbol of the Heavenly Power whom the Christians worshipped, it was manifest that Christ, the Lord of the Cross, was to be his champion and protector.[66]

Constantine's association of the Unconquered Sun with the Christian deity also explains how he could favor and endorse that deity without actually becoming a Christian. It was not unusual for Roman rulers to pay homage to multiple gods, and he continued to do so for many years.[67] He evidently did not yet grasp that the Christian divinity did not tolerate partners or competitors, and his Christian friends, grateful for his support, did not want to risk losing it by emphasizing the point. In any case, most of Constantine's subjects probably thought he *had* become a Christian. He had, after all, granted Christianity toleration, given its clergy government subsidies, and adopted a Christian emblem for the military. Moreover, soon after his victory over Maxentius, he erected a huge statue of himself holding a cross in his right hand in Rome; the inscription read in part: "By this sign of salvation, the true mark of valor, I saved your city and . . .

having freed the Senate and people of Rome, restored them to their ancient honor and glory."[68]

Licinius and the Edict of Milan

A major event that seemed to confirm Constantine's Christian leanings occurred the following year. While Constantine was now undisputed master of the western Roman sphere, the situation in the east had yet to be resolved. Galerius had recently died, leaving behind a power struggle between his nephew Maximin and Valerius Licinius, whom Galerius had appointed a fellow Augustus in 308. Constantine decided to recognize Licinius, and the two men met in Milan in February 313. They agreed to respect each other's sovereignty, and to cement the bargain Licinius married Constantine's half-sister, Constantia.

The most famous product of the meeting was the so-called Edict of Milan, granting official toleration to Christians throughout the Empire. However, the two emperors did not, as often popularly depicted, issue the document together in Milan. While the conference was in progress, news arrived that Maximin had invaded Licinius's eastern domains; departing posthaste, Licinius engaged Maximin in a furious battle on April 30 in the northern Greek region of Thrace. His forces disastrously routed, Maximin threw off his imperial array, disguised himself as a slave, and fled. On June 15, the triumphant Licinius entered Nicomedia and sent an imperial letter to the regional governor—the document later misleadingly referred to as the Edict of Milan. Since

Constantine and Licinius had agreed in their recent meeting to grant the Christians toleration, Licinius issued the letter in both their names. Thus, it began:

> When under happy auspices I, Constantine Augustus, and I, Licinius Augustus, had come to Milan and held an inquiry about all matters such as pertain to the common advantage and good . . . we resolved to issue decrees by which esteem and reverence for the Deity might be procured, that is, that we might give all Christians freedom of choice to follow the ritual which they wished.[69]

Despite the Milan agreement, the marriage, and the joint declaration of toleration, the alliance between the two emperors rapidly deteriorated. Disputes over the succession and territorial borders led to open warfare in 316, and soon afterward Licinius unexpectedly violated the toleration declaration by launching an anti-Christian persecution, giving Constantine additional motivation to oppose him. On July 3, 324, the final showdown took place at Adrianople, in Thrace. Licinius went down to defeat (suffering execution the following year), and for the next thirteen years Constantine reigned as sole emperor, the first man to rule both western and eastern Rome since Diocletian had divided the leadership in 286.

Mediator and Builder

Constantine's support for the Christians remained steadfast in the later years of his reign. His chief role in church affairs in this period was as mediator of several serious disputes that arose among the bishops, whom he recognized as the faith's political, as well as spiritual, leaders. Now that Christianity was considered a legitimate re-

---

The Edict of Milan

In his Ecclesiastical History, *the fourth-century Christian bishop Eusebius recorded the document, excerpted here, in which Licinius, Constantine's fellow emperor, announced their joint grant of religious freedom to the Christians.*

"We might give all Christians freedom of choice to follow the ritual which they wished, so that whatever is of the nature of the divine and heavenly might be propitious to us and to all those living under our authority. Accordingly, with sound and most correct reasoning we decided upon this our plan: that authority is to be refused no one at all to follow and to choose the observance or the form of worship of the Christians, and that authority be given to each one to devote his mind to that form of worship which he himself considers to be adapted to himself, in order that the Deity may be able in all things to provide for us His accustomed care and goodness."

---

ligion, it was only natural that he would assume such a role. "In the Greek and Roman state," Jones explains,

> religion was a department, and a very important one, of government. It was one of the prime duties of the government to maintain the peace of the gods. . . . The emperors considered it their duty, after due consultation with experts, to decide what was pleasing to the gods. . . . For his part Constantine had no doubts about his imperial duty. It was his task to secure God's favor on the Empire by securing, by force if necessary, that his subjects worshipped God in a manner pleasing to Him.[70]

The first church dispute the emperor arbitrated arose in 313, when Donatus, bishop of Numidia, appealed to Constantine to deny a priest named Caecilian the right to become a bishop. The Donatists, as they came to be called, argued that church officials who had caved in and handed over the Scriptures to the Romans during Diocletian's persecution were impure and immoral. Since the cleric who was to consecrate Caecilian a bishop was one of these traitors to the faith, the ceremony would be invalid. The influential bishop of Rome denounced the Donatists, as did most other bishops, and Constantine took the same position, ordering in 316 that Donatists be expelled from their churches.[71]

Much more serious and far-reaching was the controversy that arose a decade later. This became known as the Arian heresy, named after Arius, a priest of Alexandria, Egypt. As Michael Grant tells it:

> Arius seemed to be making the terrible observation that Jesus had not got quite the same qualifications as his divine Father. For what Arius maintained was that the Son, although created before time and superior to other creatures, was like them changeable . . . so that he cannot, therefore, himself be God, to whom he is in a sense posterior. That is what caused the . . . most passionate storm that ever convulsed the Christian world, since it seemed to reduce the Son to a status that was less than divine.[72]

Arianism caused such a stir among church leaders that Constantine felt compelled to intervene. He called a great council in 325 at Nicaea, not far south of Nicomedia, which over two hundred bishops attended (the first of the seven "Ecumenical Councils" held by the early church, the last also taking place in Nicaea in 787). Constantine himself sided with the majority against the Arians. He appears to have suggested that the church adopt the concept of *homoousios,* "of the same substance," essentially meaning that Christ and God were one and the same. But in spite of heated arguments both ways, the matter remained unresolved for two more centuries. To Constantine's credit, he made no move to condemn the Arians and even showed them considerable sympathy.

Another great service Constantine performed for Christianity, as well as for the Roman Empire itself, was his founding of Constantinople, "the city of Constantine." His initial reasons were probably self-glorification and the need to establish a strong base from which to defend the Empire's eastern sphere against attacks from the north and east. Its location on the Bosporus Strait (the site of the Greek town of Byzantium) was a strategically

Constantine and Eusebius at Nicaea

In this excerpt from his Life of Constantine *(quoted in Lewis and Reinhold's* Sourcebook 2*), Eusebius describes the setting of the Council of Nicaea, which he attended, and the emperor's dramatic entrance.*

"On the day fixed for the council which was to put an end to the [Arian] controversies, when the various persons who composed the synod [assembly] were at hand, in the very middle of the hall of the palace which seemed to surpass all the rest in size, there were many seats arranged in rows on both sides; and all who had been summoned entered and each sat down in his place. After the entire synod had seated itself . . . all at first fell silent, awaiting the coming of the emperor. Soon one of those closest to the emperor, then a second and third entered. . . . And when the signal was given which announced the entry of the emperor, all rose, and finally he himself approached proceeding down the center . . . dazzling the eyes of all with the splendor of his purple robe and sparkling with fiery rays, as it were, adorned for the occasion as he was with an extraordinary splendor of gold and jewels. . . . As for his soul, it was sufficiently apparent that he was adorned with the fear of God and religion."

A later European painting depicts the Council of Nicaea, in which Constantine backed the majority of bishops against the Arian heretics.

strong position for the command and defense of Thrace and Greece in the west, Asia Minor in the east, and the Black and Aegean Seas. However, because of his support of the Christians and their increasing power and influence, Constantinople also grew into a mighty Christian bastion. Indeed, at the inaugural festivities on May 11, 330, the emperor dedicated the city to the Virgin Mary and Holy Trinity.

Shortly before Easter in 337, Constantine became seriously ill and, feeling that death was near, asked to be baptized. Available evidence suggests that by this time he was a committed Christian, and the fact that he received this sacrament so late in life does not mean that he still harbored doubts about the faith. At the time, Cameron points out, "baptism was taken very seriously and it was common to defer it as late as possible so that there was less chance of committing mortal sin subsequently."[73] Eusebius, bishop of Nicomedia (not the emperor's biographer of the same name), performed the ceremony, shortly after which Constantine, whom posterity would call "the Great," died.

Thanks to Constantine's unwavering support, the Christians, though still comprising a minority of Rome's population, had a firm foothold in its religious and political spheres. Constantine's three sons—Constantine II, Constantius II, and Constans—were all pious and committed Christians. They confirmed and extended the privileges their father had given Christian clergymen, including exempting them from the poll tax, and they made bishops immune from prosecution by secular courts, allowing them to be tried by their fellow bishops. They also continued Constantine's ban on pagan sacrifices and demolished some pagan temples, although most such temples and their worship remained untouched.

The Decline of Paganism

Marring the reigns of Constantine's sons was another bloody power struggle that ended in 351 when Constantius, after killing nearly everyone in his own family, emerged victorious. He ruled as sole emperor until succumbing to sickness in 361. His successor, Julian, a distant relative who had managed to survive the family purge, was a pagan whose policies posed a potent threat to Christianity's continuing progress. He revived animal sacrifices, abolished the Christian clergy's tax exemptions, and forbade Christians from teaching rhetoric and grammar. Julian was an exceptionally intelligent, humane, and moral man. The great fourth-century Latin historian Ammianus Marcellinus said of him:

> Julian must be reckoned a man of heroic stature. . . . Philosophers tell us that there are four cardinal virtues: self-control, wisdom, justice, and courage; and, in addition to these, certain practical gifts: military skill, dignity, prosperity and generosity. All these Julian cultivated . . . with the utmost care.[74]

If Julian had lived longer, he might have slowed or stopped the growth of Christianity; most Romans were still pagans who held him in high esteem and surely would have supported him in further anti-Christian measures. However, after ruling only eighteen months, he died in 363 while campaigning against the Persians.

Julian was the Empire's last pagan emperor. The first of his Christian successors,

The emperor Julian, whose reign (360–363) was documented by the fourth-century Latin historian Ammianus Marcellinus, was Rome's last pagan ruler. Had Julian lived longer, Christianity's triumph might have been delayed.

Jovian, restored the privileges of the church, whose acquisition of new converts, political influence, land (donated by well-to-do members), and wealth resumed and greatly accelerated. Paganism now found itself increasingly under attack by zealous Christian bishops. Prominent among them was Ambrose of Milan, the most influential preacher of the late fourth century. He convinced the emperor Gratian (ruled in the west 367–383) to give up the post of *pontifex maximus,* chief priest of the state religion (traditionally held by the emperors). Urged on by Ambrose, Gratian also confiscated the funds of the state priesthood and removed the time-honored altar of the goddess Victory from the Senate House. The next emperor to come under Ambrose's persuasive influence was Theodosius I (ruled in the east 379–391; east

and west 392–395), who abolished all pagan sacrifices and cults and officially closed all pagan temples.[75]

Constantine's Revolution

At this juncture, the number of pagans in the Empire remained large and their rituals continued in secret. But many of them must have realized that their days were numbered, for Christianity undeniably had triumphed. In astonishingly little time, the church, adeptly capitalizing on the boost Constantine had given it, had managed to achieve a controlling influence over the political and religious apparatus of the Roman state. In 391, when Theodosius closed the pagan temples, no one realized, of course, that in less than a century that state would no longer exist. But Rome's demise would not deter the church, which would salvage what it could from the Empire's wreckage and go on to shape the destiny of European civilization. As the great Edward Gibbon stated it, the public establishment of Christianity was one of the most important revolutions in world history. And it was, in large degree, Constantine's revolution.

> The [military] victories and the civil policies of Constantine no longer influence the state of Europe; but a considerable portion of the globe still retains the impression which it received from the [religious] conversion of that monarch; and the ecclesiastical institutions of his reign are still connected, by an indissoluble [unbreakable] chain, with the opinions, the passions, and the interests of the present.[76]

Chapter

5 A Society in Transition: Life and Culture in the Later Empire

The political and religious upheavals caused by the rise and triumph of Christianity were perhaps the most striking aspects of cultural change in the Later Empire. But there were many others. Various economic and social factors and trends combined with the increasingly important Christian influences to determine the ongoing evolution of Roman public and private life. Most of these changes were slow and subtle, as had been the case throughout Roman history. On the surface, everyday life in Rome in the fourth and fifth centuries did not appear all that different from life in the late Republic and early Empire. Land was still Rome's main source of wealth, agriculture its major industry and source of jobs, and farming techniques and implements remained little changed since prior ages. With few exceptions, people dwelled in the same kinds of houses, villas, and apartment buildings, and still avidly flocked to arenas to see gladiatorial combats and to the circus to cheer on their favorite charioteers.

Moreover, despite its diverse mix of local peoples and languages, the Roman world's culture remained extraordinarily uniform. "The upper and middle classes all received the same type of education," A. H. M. Jones wrote,

and read the same literature, Latin in the west, and Greek in the east, and . . . wrote in the same style. . . . They all spent much of their day in the ritual of the [public] baths . . . wore the same kind of clothes, often produced in the same centers, and used the same kind of table ware. . . . The architectural appearance of any city from York [in Britain] to Gaza [in Palestine] was basically similar, and it was very difficult to distinguish a mosaic pavement on the Rhine frontier from one in Africa or Palestine.[77]

Yet beneath the surface of that empire-wide unity, the seeds of disunity were steadily growing. The most obvious of these was the struggle for religious and political dominance between Christians and pagans, which escalated throughout the fourth century. Divisiveness grew, too, within Christianity's own ranks. Besides Arianism and other doctrinal disputes, friction increased between the western clergy and their eastern brethren, foreshadowing the later split into Roman Catholic and Greek Orthodox Churches.

At the same time, the gap between rich and poor continued to widen, worsening the hardships of the lower and middle classes. The result was an overall rise in

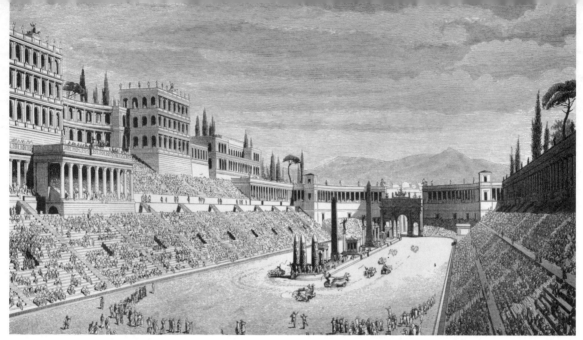

This drawing shows the huge racing stadium, the Circus Maximus—which accommodated up to a quarter of a million spectators—as it likely appeared in the third and fourth centuries.

misery and uncertainty and a corresponding decline in morale and loyalty to the state. Along with religious, ethnic, and other social tensions and disunities, such negative attitudes reflected a growing deterioration of traditional Roman values and loyalties. Though no one realized it at the time, the religious, economic, and social fabric of Roman life was undergoing a profound transformation, one that would soon bring about the end of the ancient world and the dawn of the medieval era.

A number of factors driving this steady transformation of the Roman world were economic in nature. Despite efforts by Diocletian, Constantine, and other emperors to stabilize the currency, inflation continued to rise in the fourth century, so money was usually worth very little and poverty worsened. This naturally made taxes harder to collect. Attempting to remedy the situation, the imperial government increasingly shifted this burden onto city officials. To avoid the hated job of collecting taxes, most of the talented and honest men no longer sought what had once been prestigious leadership positions.

Thus, middle- and lower-class Romans became more and more *fessi oneribus,* "exhausted by their burdens." An anonymous fourth-century writing thanking the emperor for helping a local community captures some of the financial distress and resulting agricultural devastation:

I have told, O Emperor, how much the Aeduans deserved the aid you brought them; it follows that I should tell how serious was their distress. . . . Our community lay prostrate . . . from exhaustion of resources, ever since the severity of the new tax assessment had drained our very life. . . . Indeed, a field which never meets expenses is of necessity deserted; likewise the poor country folk, staggering beneath debts, were not permitted to bring in water or cut down forests, so that whatever usable soil there was has been ruined by swamps and choked with briers . . . everything waste, uncultivated, neglected, silent, shadowy—even military roads so broken . . . that scarcely half-filled, sometimes empty wagons cross them.[78]

Some of the more desperate individuals migrated to the large cities to take advantage of the public dole. Since the early Empire, the government had maintained a policy of appeasing the poor urban masses with free handouts of bread and other foodstuffs. By the fourth century that practice had become so ingrained that eligible people regularly received food tickets, which could be passed on to one's heirs or sold to other needy people. As many as two hundred thousand people received such handouts via some twenty-three hundred distribution centers in Rome alone; Constantine extended the practice to Constantinople, which had over eighty thousand recipients by the end of his reign; and a similar system existed in Alexandria.

Other destitute people fled to the large agricultural estates and became *coloni,* tying themselves and their descendants to lives of hard labor, crushing debt, and virtual servitude. These poor tenant workers had existed during the third-century crisis, but in the Later Empire their numbers vastly increased and their condition became one of the period's most important social developments. Though not serfs in the medieval sense because they had no obligation of military service, these poor tenant workers were, Michael Grant points out, "virtually serfs—not exactly slaves, but

foreshadowing the serfdom of the Middle Ages."[79] Even after the emperor Valentinian I (reigned 364–365) abolished the poll tax, the government made sure that serfs remained bound to the land. "Lest it appear," stated one law,

> that license has been given to tenants, freed from the tie of taxation, to wander and go off where they wish, they shall be bound by the rule of origin, and though they appear to be freeborn by condition, shall nevertheless be considered as slaves of the land itself to which they are born.[80]

Tenant plots, called *colonicae,* typically consisted of a few acres each and might be farmed by one or multiple families. Within the confines of their individual restricted worlds, some *coloni* must have been more prosperous than others, since evidence suggests that a few owned a slave or two of their own.

Culture Among the Elite

Meanwhile, the rich got richer as an elite few of the old patrician-senatorial class amassed truly enormous fortunes, one of the most striking trends of the Later Empire. As the towns declined in the deteriorating economy, the rich and powerful, once mainly urban-dwelling absentee landlords, began to withdraw to their country estates. There, in Harold Mattingly's words, "they might defy the tax collector, harbor refugees from justice, and in general comport themselves as little lords. The central government was beginning to lose its grip, and something like the elements of a feudal system began to appear."[81]

Ammianus described one such noble lord, Petronius Probus, as "known all over the Roman world for his high birth, powerful influence, and vast riches; he owned estates in almost every part of the Empire, but whether they were honestly come by or not is not for a man like me to say."[82] Men like Probus evidently "came by" these estates by buying, for next to nothing, the land parcels ravaged or deserted during the devastating wars of the third and fourth centuries. On these plots they erected incredibly luxurious villas. A villa of one rural tycoon in Sicily had several courtyards, its own baths, numerous dining areas and guest bedrooms, and featured several imposing colonnades and exquisite tiled floor mosaics.

Needless to say, in sharp contrast to the squalor endured by their tenants, the owners of such palatial homes enjoyed lives of comfort and leisure. They traveled and

The Decadent Rich and Idle Poor

When he moved to Rome (from Antioch) sometime in the 380s, the historian Ammianus Marcellinus was appalled by what he viewed as a decline in the social mores of a once noble city. In this excerpt from his famous History, *he describes the vain displays of the decadent rich and the idleness of the urban poor.*

"Others think that the height of glory is to be found in unusually high carriages and an ostentatious [gaudy] style of dress; they sweat under the burden of cloaks which they attach to their necks and fasten at the throat. . . . They *contrive* by frequent movements . . . to show off their long fringes and display the garments beneath. . . . Others again, with an appearance of deep gravity, hold forth [speak] unasked on the immense extent of their family property, multiplying in imagination the annual produce of their fertile lands, which extend, they boastfully declare, from farthest east to farthest west. They presumably do not know that their ancestors, who were responsible for the expansion of Rome, did not owe their distinction to riches, but overcame all obstacles by their valor . . . in which, as far as wealth or style of living or dress was concerned, they were indistinguishable from common soldiers. . . . Of the lowest and poorest class, some spend the night in bars, others shelter under the awnings of the theaters. . . . They hold quarrelsome gambling sessions, at which they make ugly noises by breathing loudly through the nose; or else . . . they wear themselves out from dawn to dusk . . . in detailed discussion of the merits and demerits of horses and their drivers."

partied often. They also greatly enjoyed the sport of hunting, as evidenced by these comments made to a young friend by the widely influential fourth-century politician and orator Quintus Symmachus, who owned nineteen houses and estates scattered through Italy:

> I am delighted that your hunting has been so successful, that you can honor the gods and gratify your friends—the gods by nailing up antlers of stags and fangs of wild boars on the walls of their temples, your friends by sending them presents of game. . . . This is the right occupation for men of your age. . . . I shall encourage my boy to hunt as soon as he is old enough.[83]

Another popular pastime of well-to-do Romans was collecting, reading, writing, and discussing literature. It is important to realize that in that era literature was not mass-produced and widely read, as it is now. On the one hand, books had to be copied laboriously by hand and were therefore few in number and expensive; on the other, the vast majority of the population was poor and illiterate, so literary pursuits were largely a province of the upper classes. Among the favorite authors read in the fourth and fifth centuries were the literary greats of Rome's past, especially the poets Virgil and Horace, the orator Cicero, and the historian Livy, all of the first century B.C. Many also enjoyed the works of the first-century A.D. satirists Juvenal, Martial, and Persius.

Popular too in the Later Empire were contemporary authors, both secular and religious. On the secular side, Ammianus (ca. 325–395, a Greek who wrote in Latin) was the greatest historian of the age, known for his bold critiques of the ex-cesses of the privileged classes. Outstanding poets included Ausonius (ca. 310–393), Claudian (ca. 370–404), and Sidonius (ca. 430–480);[84] and Symmachus (ca. 340–402) published ten books containing over nine hundred of his letters. On the religious side were a number of noteworthy Christian literary figures. Of particular importance was Jerome (ca. 347–420), whose principal achievement was a translation of most of the Bible into Latin; his version became the vulgate, or common text, on which many of the versions of later ages were based. The religious works of Hilary (ca. 315–367), Ambrose (ca. 340–397), and Augustine (354–430) were also highly influential.

Differing Philosophies

As might be expected, most Christian writers vehemently attacked paganism. One of their most common themes was that God had placed the Roman Empire on earth as a "seedbed" for Christianity; therefore, it mattered little whether Rome survived, as long as humanity embraced God. Pagan writers responded by defending Rome and its traditional values. In a famous heated exchange between Ambrose and Symmachus, the latter called for understanding and tolerance on both sides: "What difference does it make by what pains each seeks the truth? We cannot attain to so great a secret by one road."[85] But Christian leaders increasingly recognized their own road as the only route to heavenly truths, as demonstrated by Ambrose's uncompromising reply: "You worship the works of your own hands; we think it an offense that anything which can be made should be esteemed God."[86]

One or Many Roads to the Truth?

"Symmachus:
The glory of these times makes it suitable that we defend the institutions of our ancestors and the rights and destiny of our country. . . . We demand then the restoration of that condition of religious affairs which was so long advantageous to the state. . . . It would at least have been seemly to abstain from injuring us, we beseech you, as old men to leave to posterity what we received as boys. The love of custom is great. . . . We ask, then, for peace for the gods of our fathers and of our country. It is just that all worship should be considered as one. We look on the same stars, the sky is common [to all], the same world surrounds us. What difference does it make by what pains each seeks the truth? We cannot attain to so great a secret by one road.

Ambrose:
The illustrious Prefect of the city . . . complains with sad and tearful words, asking . . . for the restoration of the rites of [the] ancient ceremonies. . . . Your sacrifice is a rite of being sprinkled with the blood of beasts. Why do you seek the voice of God in dead animals? . . . By one road, says he [Symmachus], one cannot attain to so great

Aurelius Ambrosius, commonly known as Ambrose (and later Saint Ambrose), was a provincial governor before becoming bishop of Milan in 374.

a secret. What you know not, that we know by the voice of God. And what you seek by fancies, we have found out from the very Wisdom and Truth of God. Your ways, therefore, do not agree with ours. . . . You worship the works of your own hands; we think it an offense that anything which can be made should be esteemed God. God wills not that He should be worshipped in stones."

Leisure Pursuits

Well-to-do Romans also shared some of the same leisure pursuits as the members of the lower classes. Perhaps the most common mode of relaxation, one enjoyed by Romans of nearly all walks of life, were the regular visits to the public baths, or *thermae*, that could be found in every city and town. Public bathing was a major fixture of Roman life, partly because most private residences were not equipped with bathing facilities, but more importantly because it afforded opportunities for social fellowship and the exchange of news and gossip. Even the poor could afford to go often since the entrance fee was minimal (children were admitted free). Most bathhouses either offered separate facilities for women or staggered their hours so that men and women attended at different times.[87]

The larger *thermae*, such as those built in Rome by Caracalla (early third century) and Diocletian (completed 306), were huge, beautifully decorated buildings featuring various hot and cold rooms and pools, saunas, and dressing rooms. They were also busy social centers, where people conducted business, exercised, played games, and shopped. In addition to its extensive bathing facilities, a large public bath housed massage parlors and hair salons; indoor and outdoor gyms, where people played handball and *harpastum*—a rough-and-tumble ball game similar to rugby—lifted weights, and wrestled; snack bars and gift shops; gardens for strolling and leisure conversation; and even reading rooms and libraries. Combining many features of modern malls and social clubs, the baths were places where people could enjoy themselves for a pleasant hour or an entire day.

As in earlier times, the Later Empire's two most popular public entertainments were chariot racing and gladiatorial combats. The races usually took place in long oval-shaped stadiums, the *circenses*, or circuses, the most spectacular example being the Circus Maximus in Rome, covering an area of some 2,000 by 700 feet. Huge crowds of spectators (perhaps up to 250,000) attended. Just as today's football and basketball fans cheer on their home teams, Roman racing enthusiasts rooted for factions (*factiones*), professional racing organizations represented by the colors white, red, green, and blue.[88] And successful drivers—like Flavius Scorpius, who chalked up 2,048 wins by the age of twenty-seven—became national heroes.

Equally popular were the *munera*. These shows, featuring fights between gladiators, men and beasts, or beasts and beasts, generally took place in amphitheaters like Rome's enormous and luxurious Colosseum. The gladiators first raised their weapons to the highest-ranking official present and recited the phrase *"Morituri te salutamus!"* or "We who are about to die salute you!" Then they fought, usually to the death. In other shows, low-level gladiators known as *bestiarii*, or "beast men," hunted and slaughtered animals, including tigers, bears, and elephants, to the delight of the spectators.

Many Romans also engaged in various kinds of gambling, including dice-tossing and *micatio*. In the latter, still played in Italy as the game *morra*, at a given signal two players simultaneously revealed random numbers of fingers while shouting out guesses as to what the total number of fingers would be. The player whose guess came the closest won the round along with whatever had been wagered. Large

This first-century A.D. terracotta plaque shows a quadrigarum, *a four-horse chariot, speeding toward the turning posts at the end of the racetrack's* spina, *or central axis. A single horseman, partially visible at right, rides ahead, setting the race's frantic pace.*

numbers of people also regularly participated in betting pools on sporting events, especially chariot races. And there was always plenty of heavy betting on cockfighting, a pastime extremely popular among the lower classes but also pursued by some of the well-to-do, particularly military types. By the fourth century, gambling had become so common in Roman cities, especially Rome, that on a visit to that city Ammianus professed surprise that the practice was so widespread and open among people of all classes. "Some of these people," he wrote about upperclass gamblers,

> dislike the name of gamblers and prefer to be called dice-players, though the distinction is no more than that between a thief and a robber. It must be admitted, however, that, while all other friendships at Rome are lukewarm, those between gamblers are as close

and are maintained with as much steadfast affection as if they had been forged by common effort in a glorious cause.[89]

An Emphasis on Moral Behavior

Pastimes such as gambling and attending the baths and races continued until the Empire's official end in 476 (and well beyond, for daily life went on as before under Rome's early barbarian leaders). Yet attitudes about these activities began to change during Christianity's ascendancy in the early fourth century. Christian leaders increasingly came to condemn these and many other traditional Roman customs. As Professor Jones phrased it, "The theater, gladiatorial shows, wild beast fights, and even horse racing were all sinful, and the baths were deprecated [disapproved of] as an indulgence liable to stimulate the carnal [sexual] appetites."[90]

The Christians especially disliked the gladiatorial combats, which they viewed as murder. Fourth-century Christian bishops echoed the powerful words of their respected predecessor, the second-century Christian apologist Tertullian: "He who shudders at the body of a man who died of natural causes . . . will in the amphitheater, gaze down with the most tolerant eyes on the bodies of men mangled, torn to pieces, defiled with their own blood."[91] Influential bishops, including Ambrose, pressed the emperors to ban arena combats. And these efforts eventually succeeded, despite the protests of Roman pagans, who still made up a large proportion of the population; sometime in the 390s, the government closed the gladiatorial schools, although the combats themselves went on until about 440. The amphitheaters remained open and widely popular, however. As late as 523, half a century after the last Roman emperor vacated the throne, the Colosseum still drew huge crowds to watch wild beast hunts and wrestling matches.

Conservative Christian views also began to permeate other social areas, including private life. The traditional Roman gods had rarely intruded into people's personal affairs; however, the Christian god, at least as portrayed by clergymen like Ambrose and Augustine, was deeply concerned with the behavior, attitudes, and even the thoughts of individual humans. "Their sexual behavior seemed of particular concern to Him," writes Charles Freeman.

> It was perhaps at this moment [the late fourth and early fifth centuries] that intense guilt replaced public shame as a conditioner of moral behavior. Ever more lurid descriptions of the horrors of hell accompanied the shift. Soon consuming fires and devils with red-hot instruments of torture entered European mythology.[92]

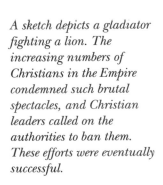

A sketch depicts a gladiator fighting a lion. The increasing numbers of Christians in the Empire condemned such brutal spectacles, and Christian leaders called on the authorities to ban them. These efforts were eventually successful.

Some earlier Christian thinkers, notably Origen (third century), had argued that God was too good and compassionate to condemn people to such a terrible place as hell, but leading Christian thinkers of the Later Empire, Augustine the most prominent among them, rejected this view and warned that sin would lead to eternal

Vast Sums Poured into Building Churches

One of the most visible changes in Roman life in the fourth and fifth centuries was the rapid proliferation of Christian churches, as summarized here by historian Charles Freeman in The World of the Romans.

"Early Christian communities were forced to meet in private houses. . . . By the 3rd century, with numbers of converts growing, a whole house might be adopted as a church, with a large meeting room and separate rooms for baptism and clergy. . . . Once Constantine's Edict of Milan proclaimed toleration . . . for Christianity . . . this all changed. The emperor poured vast sums of money into his church building program and all over the Empire new churches appeared, resplendent with their fine decoration. . . . Many were built over the shrines of martyrs, places which had been venerated since the early days of the church. Others took over prime sites within the major cities—even the sites of earlier imperial palaces—while Constantinople was planned as a Christian city. Churches now became magnificent treasure houses, objects of awe and inspiration of worship. . . . [For their design] there was a pagan model to copy: the basilica, typically a long hall with a flat timber roof and aisles running along its length. For centuries the basilicas had been used as law courts . . . or [as] places to meet and gossip. Now they were to receive a new function. . . . The greatest of the basilicas was St. Peter's in Rome, constructed over the shrine which for generations was believed to be the resting place of St. Peter's body. A vast terrace was leveled on the Vatican Hill and the basilica when built was 119 meters [391 feet] long and 64 meters [210 feet] wide. . . . The inner aisles of the nave [central hall] were marked off by 44 huge columns of marble taken from earlier Roman buildings and the whole building was decorated with beautiful objects of gold and silver."

punishment. Augustine also strongly advocated the doctrine of original sin, the idea that Adam and Eve's transgressions in the Garden of Eden had condemned all people to begin life as sinners. Only by gaining God's grace through the sacrament of baptism, said Augustine, could a person be accepted into heaven. After heated arguments with other Christian leaders, Augustine managed to get the emperor Honorius (reigned 395–423) to force western bishops to make the principle official church doctrine.

The Christian Ethic

This heavy emphasis on moral behavior, sin, and punishment naturally affected social mores and customs, including marriage, divorce, and the treatment of women. In preceding centuries, women had made important strides toward emancipation in what was, from first to last, a highly male-dominated society. They gained the right, for example, to sue for divorce at will and to remarry after a one-year waiting period (divorced men could remarry immediately). However, this changed when, in 331, under pressure from Christian bishops, Constantine passed a law that forbade women from seeking divorce for reasons such as adultery, physical abuse, or gambling; the only grounds now acceptable were murder or tomb-robbing by their husbands.[93] The law also restricted men; though they *could* sue their wives for adultery, that, along with poisoning and procuring prostitutes, were the only acceptable grounds. As Christianity's grip on Roman society grew stronger, people increasingly viewed women as objects of sexual temptation for men; female virginity as a treasured virtue; and sex, except by a married couple attempting to create children, as a sin.

It must be stressed that many of the changes in social attitudes wrought by the Christian revolution in the Later Empire were concerned less with restricting personal behavior and more with making society more humane and equitable. Christian preachers and teachers urged people to be humble, self-sacrificing, nonviolent, and kind. Moreover, they insisted that such kindness should be extended to the realm's most miserable and desperate inhabitants—the poor, the sick, slaves, and even prisoners. As Christianity's ranks grew, and more Romans accepted these ideas, providing charity to society's poor and powerless became a large-scale, widely accepted activity. According to Averil Cameron:

> Already in the third century the church of Rome maintained some eighteen hundred widows, orphans, and poor by its charity; in fourth-century Antioch, three thousand widows and virgins were registered, quite apart from needy men. . . . The idea of giving to the poor was an important part of the Christian ethic, and such charity might also take the form of individual renunciation [of wealth]. . . . Wealthy Christians sold up their estates on a vast scale, giving the proceeds to local churches, making provision for feeding the poor on a regular basis, or giving them direct distributions of money.[94]

The Roman emperors, mostly Christians from Constantine's time on, reflected these more humane attitudes in some of their social legislation. A striking example was a ban on infanticide, or killing babies.

Since Rome's earliest days, fathers, through their right of *patria potestas,* or complete authority over their families, had routinely exposed handicapped or unwanted children to the elements. Christians viewed this as murder, and a law passed in 374 labeled it as such.

An Age of Contrasts

Laws providing for more lenient treatment of slaves were another result of Christianity's softening effect on the harsher aspects of Roman institutions. For instance, Constantine ruled that slaves condemned to the mines or arena should be branded on the legs or arms instead of the face (as had been the prior practice) and that the murder of a slave was as serious a crime as killing a freeman and should receive the same penalty. He also passed a law forbidding the division of slave families being sold:

> When . . . estates in Sardinia were recently distributed among the various present proprietors, the division of holdings ought to have been made in such a way that a whole family of slaves would remain with one individual landholder. For who could tolerate that children should be separated from parents, sisters from brothers, and wives from husbands? . . . Take pains that throughout the province no complaint shall hereafter persist over the separation of the loved ones of slaves.[95]

Beyond these and similar measures, Christian leaders in the Later Empire basically accepted slavery as an entrenched and inevitable institution. Augustine recognized that slavery was evil in principle, but he saw no alternative to it and preached that slaves would receive special rewards in the afterlife for their earthly sufferings.

That the lot of slaves improved somewhat while millions of poor farmers (the *coloni*) sank deeper into hopeless servitude is one of the many ironies and contradictions that characterized life in the Later Empire. The Roman world had always been a place of glaring contrasts, in Grant's words "both wonderful and horrible, as startling and enlightened in many ways as it was gray and brutish in others."[96] Now those contrasts seemed to sharpen. Many of the merely rich became fabulously rich while many of the poor became truly destitute; some aristocrats mercilessly exploited the peasants while others generously donated their fortunes to them; the bishops preached that God's love is boundless while warning that he sends some people to hell. Clearly, Roman society was undergoing a major transformation from the inside out. What it might have become if left alone we will never know; for even as it struggled to put its house in order, the barbarians had begun to press, with irresistible force, from the outside in.

6 Into the Realm of Legend: The Fall of the Western Empire

Some modern historians have characterized many of the economic, social, and religious changes that occurred in the Later Empire as signs of the decay of Roman civilization, contributing heavily to its eventual fall. They cite, for instance, overall economic decline; the migration of many of the wealthy from the cities to the countryside, where they could better evade government control; growing religious and political divisions between pagans and Christians; the changes in traditional Roman institutions and customs wrought by Christian influences; and increasing administrative corruption and social apathy. But recent scholarship has come to see these factors more as part of Rome's continuing evolution than as agents of its doom. From this point of view, they were merely temporary setbacks in the Empire's struggle to reinvent itself after the setbacks of the third century.

The strongest evidence suggests that what ultimately did Rome in was a long series of pounding blows by invading barbarian tribes, coupled with an increasing inability of Roman armies to repel these intruders. The French historian André Piganiol aptly summed it up in the now-famous phrase, "Roman civilization did not die a natural death. It was murdered."[97] Arther Ferrill concurs and adds

that the Empire unwittingly contributed to its own demise by allowing its military to deteriorate in size and quality in its final century. "After 410," he writes,

> the emperor in the West could no longer project military power to the ancient frontiers. That weakness led immediately to the loss of Britain and within a generation to the loss of Africa. . . . The shrinkage of the imperial frontiers from 410 to 440 was directly the result of military conquests by barbarian forces . . . and Rome fell to the onrush of barbarism.[98]

It should be emphasized that this fall took place only in the west. For various economic, strategic, and manpower reasons, the eastern Empire, centered at Constantinople, was able to weather the storm that lashed and finally sank the west. Also, the fall of the western Empire was not a sudden event. It was instead a gradual disintegration, beginning with the major barbarian incursions of the late fourth century, and later encompassing the steady loss of territory throughout the fifth century and the dethroning of the last western emperor in 476.

Who were these intruders who managed to topple the greatest empire the world had ever seen? According to Piganiol, they were loosely organized tribal

Fierce, skilled Germanic horsemen like these early Gauls played a crucial role in the long series of frontier incursions and battles that eventually brought about the disintegration of the Roman Empire.

threatened Rome throughout its development. One group of invaders, the Gauls, had ravaged northern Italy in the 390s B.C. And when the Teuton and Cimbri tribes had assaulted Rome's western provinces in 108 B.C., it had required the greatest general of the age, Marius, to beat them back. A century later, hoping to create a buffer zone between these marauders and the Roman heartland, Augustus, the first emperor, extended Roman borders northward to the Danube. His troops encountered stiff resistance from several northern European tribes, by now collectively referred to as Germans. The first-century A.D. historian Tacitus described the Germanic peoples as "wild," with "blue eyes, reddish hair and huge frames." About their formidable warriors, he wrote:

> Only a few use swords or lances. The spears that they carry—*framaea* is the native word—have short and narrow heads, but are so sharp and easy to handle that the same weapon serves at need for close or distant fighting. The [barbarian] horseman asks no more than his shield and spear. . . . They are either naked or only lightly clad in their cloaks. . . . Few have breastplates; only here and there will you see a helmet of metal or hide.[100]

peoples who "had a primitive economy . . . were ignorant of coinage . . . [and] had a rudimentary alphabet. But they were born soldiers. . . . The chief was surrounded by faithful men who wanted to die bravely for him."[99] It is no coincidence that the phrases "born soldiers," "faithful men," and "die bravely" also fittingly describe the sturdy Roman soldiers who had earlier conquered the Mediterranean world. Ironically, these tribesmen, whom the Romans so disparagingly called barbarians, were their distant cousins. Periodic mass migrations of nomadic peoples from western Asia into Europe had occurred for millennia; and the classical Greeks and Romans were the descendants of some of the earliest European arrivals.

This process had never actually ceased, as new waves of northern nomads had

For a while, Augustus seemed on the verge of conquering and Romanizing the Germans. But when a Roman army was annihilated in a northern forest in A.D. 9, he backed off, a failure that haunted his successors. The barbarian incursions Marcus Aurelius had to deal with in the second century and the attacks by the Goths and others in the third century might have been avoided had the Empire by those times stretched to the shores of the North Sea.

Military Deterioration

Thus, the climactic barbarian onslaughts of the fourth and fifth centuries were part of a long-established and still-ongoing process. But there were important differences between these invasions and those of the past. First, they were immensely larger in scope. Second, the Roman armies sent to repel them were increasingly inadequate to the task, in part because many of the soldiers manning these armies were now barbarians themselves. The "barbarization" of the Roman military had begun in prior centuries when the government had allowed Germans from the northern frontier areas to settle in Roman lands. The Roman government often followed this more peaceful policy partly because it realized that most barbarian groups wanted to *become* Romans, not destroy them. Stewart Perowne explains:

> The tribesmen . . . had no desire whatsoever to set up their own fragmentary states. What they wanted was to enter the Roman state, the sole repository of civilization and wealth. If necessary they would do it by force; but if they could do it peacefully, and get paid for it into the bargain, so much the better. Thus we find an increasing military intake from foreign [barbarian] nations and whole groups of foreigners settled within Roman frontiers at their own request.[101]

Once these settlers had established themselves, they were more than willing to fight Rome's enemies, including fellow Germans. And Roman leaders, always in need of tough military recruits, took advantage of that fact.

However, as the recruitment of Germans into the military accelerated, this policy began to take its toll, particularly in a loss of discipline, traditionally one of the Roman army's greatest strengths. According to Ferrill:

> The use of Germans on such a large scale that the army became German rather than the Germans becoming Roman soldiers, begins with Theodosius [in the late fourth century]. . . . His Gothic allies . . . began immediately to demand great rewards for their service and to show an independence that in drill, discipline and organization meant catastrophe. They fought

A Roman general (right) is accompanied by his Germanic standard bearer. The so-called barbarization of the Roman army was a gradual process that occurred over several centuries.

under their own native commanders, and the barbaric system of discipline was in no way as severe as the Roman. Eventually Roman soldiers saw no reason to do what barbarian troops in Roman service were rewarded heavily for not doing. . . . Too long and too close association with barbarian warriors, as allies in the Roman army, had ruined the qualities that made Roman armies great. . . . The Roman army of A.D. 440, in the West, had become little more than a barbarian army itself.[102]

A gradual breakdown in discipline was not the only factor contributing to the erosion of the Later Empire's military. The soldiers were paid very little and, because of the government's frequent money problems, their wages were often months or even years in arrears, which damaged morale. Lack of military funding, in combination with other factors, also affected the quality of weapons and armor. "By the end of the fourth century," writes Ferrill, "weapons and weapons training had deteriorated drastically."[103]

In addition, the Roman army grew steadily smaller, partly because of difficulties in recruiting in the western provinces, which were less populous than the eastern ones, and also because some Christians refused to fight. Perhaps the chief factor, however, was that large numbers of men found ways—legal or illegal—of avoiding service. "Hosts of Senators, bureaucrats and clergymen were entitled to avoid the draft," Michael Grant points out,

and among other groups who escaped [legally] were cooks, bakers and slaves. To draw the rest of the population into the levy, the combing-out process was intensive. Even the men in the em-peror's own very extensive estates found themselves called up. Yet other great landlords proved far less cooperative. They were supposed to furnish army recruits in proportion to the size of their lands. But on many occasions they resisted firmly.[104]

Moreover, because of low pay and the physical hardships of service, some young men resorted to extreme measures, such as amputating their own thumbs, to dodge the draft. When this practice became widespread, the government at first ordered that such shirkers be burned alive; later, as the need for new soldiers became more desperate, the authorities spared self-mutilated men from the stake but forced them to serve in the army despite their handicap.

The Downward Spiral Begins

Periodic staggering battle losses also contributed to the reduction in both the numbers and morale of Roman troops in the Later Empire. Some of the most serious losses occurred during the civil disputes among Constantine's sons in the mid–fourth century and Julian's unsuccessful Persian campaign in 363. Much worse, though, was a major defeat suffered by Roman forces immediately following the first of the massive final series of barbarian incursions. The trouble began in about 370, when the Huns, a fierce nomadic people from central Asia, swept into eastern Europe, driving the Goths and other German tribes into the Roman border provinces. Ammianus's graphic description of the Huns explains why they

An engraving depicting the arrival of the Huns in eastern Europe. The Latin historian Ammianus disparagingly called them "prodigiously ugly" people who ate raw animal flesh and never washed, but he also gave them their due as highly skilled and effective mounted warriors.

appeared repulsive and frightening even to the Germanic barbarians.

> [The Huns] are quite abnormally savage. . . . They have squat bodies, strong limbs, and thick necks, and are so prodigiously ugly and bent that they might be two-legged animals, or the figures [gargoyles] crudely carved from stumps which are seen on the parapets of bridges. . . . Their way of life is so rough that they have no use for fire or seasoned food, but live on the roots of wild plants and the half-raw flesh of any sort of animals, which they warm a little by placing it between their thighs and the backs of their horses. They have no buildings to shelter them, but avoid anything of the kind as carefully as we avoid living in the neighborhood of tombs. . . . Once they have put their necks into some dingy shirt they never take it off or change it till it rots and falls to pieces. . . . When they join battle they advance in packs, uttering their various war-cries. Being lightly equipped and very sudden in their movements they can deliberately scatter and gallop about at random, inflicting tremendous slaughter.[105]

The advance of the Huns set in motion the greatest folk migrations in history, as the Goths, Vandals, Burgundians, Franks, Angles, Alani, Saxons, and many other tribes spread over Europe in search of new lands. As many as two hundred thousand members of one branch of the Goths, the Visigoths (meaning "wise Goths"), poured across the Danube into Rome's northeastern provinces. The eastern emperor, Valens, allowed these refugees to settle,

Death Knell of the Roman Cause

"Amid the clashing of arms and weapons on every side . . . sounding the death-knell of the Roman cause, our retreating troops rallied with shouts of mutual encouragement. But, as the fighting spread like fire and numbers of them were transfixed by arrows and whirling javelins, they lost heart. Then the opposing lines came into collision like ships of war and pushed each other to and fro, heaving under the reciprocal motion like the waves of the sea. Our left wing penetrated as far as the very wagons [of the enemy camp] . . . but it was abandoned by the rest of the cavalry, and under pressure of numbers gave way and collapsed like a broken dike. This left the infantry unprotected and so closely huddled together that a man could hardly wield his sword or draw back his arm once he had stretched it out. Dust rose in such clouds as to hide the sky, which rang with frightful shouts. . . . The barbarians poured on in huge columns, trampling down horse and man and crushing our ranks so as to make an orderly retreat impossible. Our men were too close-packed to have any hope of escape; so they resolved to die like heroes, faced the enemy's swords, and struck back at their assailants. . . . In this mutual slaughter so many were laid low that the field was covered with the bodies of the slain, while the groans of the dying and severely wounded filled all who heard them with abject fear."

perhaps hoping to recruit their warriors for his army. However, his representatives unwisely insulted and tried to exploit the Visigoths, who responded by pillaging their way through the province of Thrace. Valens hastened with an army to put down this uprising. But instead of waiting for reinforcements from his nephew, the western emperor Gratian, he imprudently attacked the much larger enemy force on his own near Adrianople, in eastern Thrace. On that dark day for Rome, August 9, 378, the overconfident Valens died along with at least two-thirds of his army.[106] When news of the catastrophe reached Italy, Ambrose called it "the massacre of all humanity, the end of the world."[107]

Ambrose had exaggerated, for this one defeat, though crippling, was not enough to bring down the Empire. Yet his words bore an element of truth. In a way the disaster at Adrianople marked a crucial turning point for Rome, the beginning of a military-political downward spiral that would eventually seal its fate. Moreover, what would ultimately prove a more critical turn in barbarian-Roman affairs occurred soon afterward. Gratian appointed the respected army general Theodosius to succeed Valens. In 382 Theodosius negotiated a deal with the Visigoths, allowing them to settle in Thrace permanently. In return for providing troops for the Roman army, they were free from taxation and could serve under their own leaders, making them *foederati,* "federates," or equal allies living within the Empire. This set an ominous precedent for the future. As Charles Freeman puts it, "This was the first time that an area within the borders of the Empire had been passed out of effective Roman control."[108]

An Empire in Disarray

Over the next several decades, one barbarian tribe after another acquired federate status in the western provinces, a trend that steadily weakened the western Empire both politically and militarily. On the one hand, the Roman government lost much of its authority over an increasing amount of territory. On the other, large numbers of warriors from these tribes joined the Roman army, which, in consequence, suffered a continued reduction in discipline and effectiveness. Despite these problems,

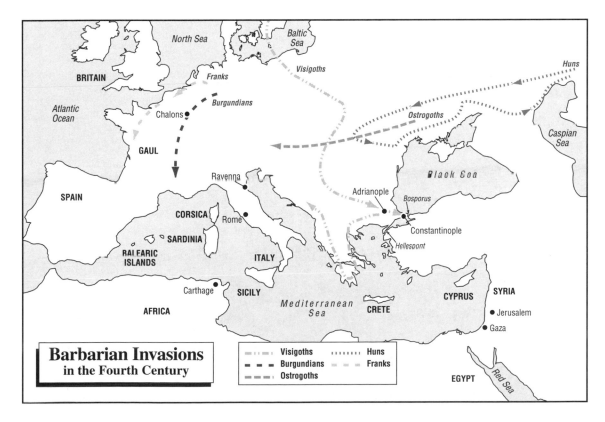

Barbarian Invasions in the Fourth Century

	Visigoths		Huns
	Burgundians		Franks
	Ostrogoths		

the emperors actually welcomed these recruits, partly because of heavy military losses sustained in crushing a series of rebellions by imperial usurpers in the late fourth and early fifth centuries.

The Empire also badly needed troops to deal with growing threats from various barbarian groups, each demanding its own piece of the Roman pie. Theodosius, the last emperor to rule over both eastern and western spheres, died in 395. His sons, Honorius, age eleven, and Arcadius, seventeen, assumed the western and eastern thrones, respectively, and thereafter the governments and national policies of the two spheres became distinct enough to make Rome a *partes imperii,* an empire consisting of two independent parts.

This new situation deeply worried the Visigoths. Apparently they thought that the deal they had struck with Theodosius might only be valid under his rule; now that he was dead and the Empire divided, they might be vulnerable. So they banded together under a strong leader, Alaric, and began making demands. When the Romans refused to comply, they plundered Thrace. And a few years later, in about 402, they marched on Italy, where Honorius's army, commanded by the capable barbarian general Stilicho, halted their advance.

These bold actions by Alaric and his Visigoths turned out to have indirect effects that proved more disruptive and dangerous for the Empire than his own attacks. To meet the Visigothic threat, Honorius had to recall several legions from Britain. Almost immediately, the tribal Picts of Scotland began raiding southward, while the Saxons and other Germanic tribes crossed the North Sea and raided Roman British towns and farms. At the same time, encouraged by Alaric's partial success, another tribe in-

The German-born Roman general Stilicho (ca. 365–408), who virtually ruled the western section of the Empire as Honorius's regent, negotiates with a group of Visigoths. Though successful on the battlefield, Stilicho was later accused of treason and executed.

vaded northern Italy, and in 406 fierce Vandal, Alani, and Suevi armies swept through Gaul, some of them continuing on into Rome's Spanish provinces. Stilicho managed to defeat the invaders in Italy. But because western Rome now lacked the resources to stop them, those who had entered Gaul and Spain stayed permanently. In 407, after the last legions were recalled from Britain, the island fell under the control of native and Germanic peoples.

With the western Empire seemingly in disarray, in 408 Alaric regrouped his forces and once more moved on Italy. This time he was able to march straight to Rome almost unopposed. Rome was no longer the imperial capital, of course, but it was still the Empire's largest city and the chief symbol of more than a thousand years of Roman power and prestige.[109] Surely, Alaric reasoned, threatening to sack it would force Honorius to meet his demands. About these demands, noted scholar Peter Heather writes:

> At most, he [Alaric] offered a military alliance with the Roman state, demanding, in return, a generalship for himself, a large annual payment in gold, substantial corn supplies, and his troops to be settled in the Venetias and Raetia [key provinces lying directly north of Italy]. Such a position would have allowed the Goths to control Ravenna [in northeastern Italy, then the western Roman capital] and routes over the Alps. The level of ambition here is remarkable. . . . The envisaged proximity of Alaric's force to [Rome's] political heart would have effectively established a Gothic protectorate [position of superior authority] over the western Empire.[110]

When the Roman government rejected these audacious demands, Alaric besieged and in 410 sacked Rome, an event that sent shock waves through the Mediterranean world. Jerome, who was then living in Palestine, spoke for many when he said, "My voice is stopped, and sobs cut off the words as I try to speak. Captive is the city which once took captive all the world. . . . The city of old . . . is fallen to ruin . . . and everywhere is the specter of death."[111] In reality, Rome had suffered relatively little ruin and death. Alaric's men had plundered much gold and other valuables but had stayed only three days and done little physical damage. Some murders and rapes had occurred, but many of these appear to have been committed by Roman slaves taking advantage of the crisis to exact revenge on their masters.

Ancient Prophecy and the Scourge of God

Not surprisingly, many pagans blamed the great city's sacking on Christianity's denial of the traditional Roman gods. This charge motivated Augustine to pen *The City of God,* in which he claimed that the pagans' own sins had brought about the disaster. Others looked to ancient prophecy for an explanation of the Empire's increasing troubles. According to one of the traditional founding legends, shortly before establishing Rome, Romulus had seen twelve eagles flying together; later generations of Romans passed along a superstition that each of these birds symbolized a century of the nation's existence. In the year 447, many noted, the twelve hundred years of the prophecy would be up. This, they said, might explain why the Roman world seemed to be falling apart.

For those who accepted this ancient prophecy, the Empire's continuing downward spiral in the years following Alaric's capture of Rome only confirmed their worst fears. In particular, the rise of an unusually fierce and powerful Hunnish king, Attila, in the 430s appeared to many Romans to signal the approaching apocalypse. By this time the Huns had built up an immense empire stretching from southern Russia westward across northern Europe to the Danube River. Living up to his nickname, the "Scourge of God," Attila ravaged various eastern and western Roman provinces for years, striking terror into the hearts and lives of millions. Finally, in about 450, he demanded to be given half of the western Roman realm. When the Romans refused this demand, he marched his huge army into Gaul and began burning and sacking cities. Luckily for the Empire, in the following year a combined army of Romans, Visigoths, and other German federates, led by the last great Roman general, Aetius, met and routed the Hunnish forces near Chalons, in what is now northern France. Two years later, Attila died unexpectedly and, as J. B. Bury memorably put it, "the empire of the Huns . . . was soon scattered to the winds."[112]

The West More Vulnerable than the East

Attila's rampages had not only caused much death, destruction, and social chaos in the west, but also demonstrated that the west was much more vulnerable to attack and devastation than the east. Attila had assaulted and looted the east's Danubian provinces, lying west of Constantinople, but he had eventually thought twice about confronting that city's massive walls and fleets and prudently switched his attention to the western realm. "If the western emperor failed to hold any part of the Rhine and Danube fronts," A. H. M. Jones explained,

> he had no second line of defense; the invaders could penetrate straight into Italy and Gaul, and even into Spain. The eastern emperor, if he failed, as he often did, to hold the lower Danube, only lost control temporarily of the [Danubian provinces]; for no enemy could force the Bosporus and the Hellespont [straits], guarded by Constantinople itself. Asia Minor, Syria, and Egypt thus remained sealed off from invasion.[113]

Besides its strategic advantage over the west, the east enjoyed more political stability and had far fewer internal rebellions to deal with. The eastern realm also possessed considerably more wealth and a larger population, which meant that it could more easily recruit and maintain troops.

These differences between eastern and western Rome became more and more telling as the west continued to deteriorate. In 455 the city of Rome suffered the indignity of a second capture, this time by the Vandals. They had previously crossed from Spain into Africa, overrun Rome's fertile North African provinces, which produced much of the western Empire's grain, and gained federate status. These actions had in no way threatened the livelihood and stability of the eastern Empire, which imported most of its grain from Egypt. Now, with Italy seemingly at their mercy, the Vandals, led by their bold and capable king, Gaiseric, sailed north and ransacked Rome for fourteen days before departing.

Divine Intervention or Weird Coincidence?

The western Empire had by now shrunk to a pale ghost of the mighty state of the *Pax Romana* days. The last few western emperors, all of them weak and ineffectual rulers, reigned over a pitiful realm consisting only of the Italian peninsula and portions of a few nearby provinces. Even these lands were not safe or secure, partly because barbarian claims on Roman territory continued and also because what was left of the once powerful Roman army was quickly disintegrating. The military situation in the northern province of Noricum, for which evidence survives, serves to illustrate a process that must have been taking place almost everywhere in the west. "As late as the 470s," Freeman writes,

there were still army units stationed in the main cities of the province. At one point their pay failed to arrive. One unit sent off a delegation to Italy to collect the money but no more was heard of it and the unit disbanded itself. Others followed and the defense of the frontier was, in effect, disbanded. Germans soon moved over the frontier to take control.[114]

Roman Swan Song

This tract from the Voyage Home to Gaul *(quoted in Duff and Duff,* Minor Latin Poets*) was composed circa 416 by the poet Rutilius Namatianus. Because it sings the praises of traditional Rome, suggesting that some Romans still held out hope for the Empire's survival and resurgence, the piece is often referred to as "Rome's swan song."*

"Listen, O fairest queen of your world, Rome, welcomed amid the starry skies, listen, you mother of men and mother of gods, thanks to your temples we are not far from heaven: you do we chant [the praises of], and shall, while destiny allows, forever chant [them]. . . . Sooner shall guilty oblivion overwhelm the sun than the honor due to you quit my heart: for your benefits extend as far as the sun's rays, where the circling Ocean-flood bounds the world. . . . For nations far apart you have made a single fatherland; under your dominion captivity has meant profit even for those who knew not justice: and by offering to the vanquished a share in your own justice, you have made a city of what was formerly a world. . . . Spread forth the laws that are to last throughout the ages of Rome: alone you need not dread the distaffs of the Fates. . . . The span [of Rome's reign] which remains is subject to no bounds, so long as earth shall stand firm and heaven uphold the stars!"

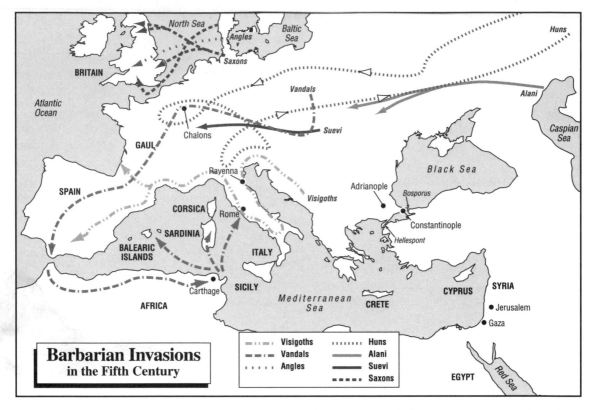

Barbarian Invasions
in the Fifth Century

Visigoths		Huns
Vandals		Alani
Angles		Suevi
		Saxons

Not long after the delegation from Noricum made its unsuccessful journey, Ravenna, refuge of the last feeble vestiges of imperial power in the west, itself came under German control. By this time, practically all of the Roman troops still active in Italy were German mercenary warriors, mostly Heruls, Rugians, and Scirians from eastern Europe, led by German officers. In the summer of 476 they demanded what Rome had granted to so many other barbarian groups in the recent past—federate status. Further, they wanted one-third of the land in Italy to create their own domain. The government refused, setting in motion the swift, final, and fatal chain of events. The troops rebelled, proclaimed their officer Odoacer as their king, then promptly marched into Ravenna and ousted Romulus Augustulus,

the unremarkable young man who then occupied the western throne. The western imperial government, which had been barely functioning for decades, now simply ceased to exist.

When the news of these events spread through the rest of Italy, some noted with superstitious awe that the Roman state had lasted for a total of 1,229 years, a span almost exactly matching the twelve centuries of the ancient prophecy. Was this the work of divine intervention, either by the old pagan gods or the new Christian one? Or was it just a strange, perverse coincidence? No one could say for sure. What would become more certain in the ensuing years was that, while the city of Rome still stood, the western Empire, once undisputed master of the Mediterranean world, had passed forever into the realm of legend.

The Living Legacy of Rome

Although no emperor took Romulus Augustulus's place when he vacated the imperial throne in 476, marking the end of the traditional Roman state, everyday life in Italy and other parts of the west went on as usual. Indeed, no significant administrative or social upheaval accompanied the transition to barbarian rule, and the first few Germanic kings who succeeded Augustulus strove their best to maintain continuity and show respect for most Roman traditions and institutions. Like many earlier barbarians, they admired Roman civilization and wanted to become part of it, rather than to destroy it. According to the late and noted historian Ferdinand Lot:

> None of the great events, such as the invasions of the barbarians . . . the disappearance of the "Empire" in 476, the arrival of the Goths and their occupation of the country, affected deeply the social life or even the organization and administrative geography of the country. People imagine, or rather used to imagine, some mysterious revolution in 476 which was not merely political but also social. . . . Things did not, however, happen in this way. . . . There was still a Senate . . . [and] a Prefect of Rome [although neither wielded any real power]. . . .

Rome was still the finest city of the West. The sight of it struck strangers and even the barbarians with admiration. It went on, moreover, with its life of idleness; there was no intermission of the circus and amphitheater games. It does not, in truth, appear that the Italian populace had to make any real changes in its habits.[115]

Thus, the transition from ancient to medieval society in Europe, in which the barbarian kingdoms absorbed much of Rome's culture, was a slow and gradual process that occurred over many generations.

Rome Under the Barbarians

The degree of continuity between imperial and barbarian rule is well illustrated by the reign of Theodoric the Ostrogoth, who defeated and succeeded Odoacer in 493. Theodoric was such a humane and sympathetic ruler that one contemporary writer compared him with Trajan, one of the five "good" emperors of the *Pax Romana* era. The Senate, still the main symbol and mouthpiece of the Roman aristocracy, received the utmost respect from Theodoric. Collaborating with many of these nobles, he restored a number of the public buildings destroyed by the Vandals and other invaders and made a serious effort to replenish the state treasury.[116] Another way he showed respect for Roman ways and institutions was to appoint Romans to nearly all civilian posts.[117]

Most significant, Theodoric strove to maintain Roman *civilitas,* roughly translated as the preservation of basic liberties under Roman law. In about 500, he reaffirmed the Theodosian Code, a collection, made by the eastern emperor Theodosius II (reigned 408–450), of imperial laws issued since the early fourth century. Summarizing Theodoric's largely enlightened reign, the sixth-century Byzantine historian Procopius wrote:

> Theodoric was an extraordinary lover of justice, and adhered rigorously to the laws. He guarded the country from barbarian invasions, and displayed the greatest intelligence and prudence. There was in his government scarcely a trace of injustice towards his subjects, nor would he permit any of those under him to attempt anything of the kind. . . . Thus then Theodoric was in name a "tyrant," but in truth a true king, not inferior to the best of his predecessors, and his popularity grew greatly, both among Goths and Italians.[118]

Despite such enthusiastic accounts, Theodoric and other barbarian rulers did not absorb and pass on Rome's national spirit, ideals, and notion of a grand empire encompassing many diverse peoples. Their dominions consisted of small, largely disunited and backward kingdoms that frequently fought one another. Moreover, as A. H. M. Jones explains, they

Upon entering Rome in the year 500, Theodoric, a largely humane and constructive ruler, receives a warm welcome from the reigning pope, Symmachus, and members of the Senate.

combined the characteristic vices of the Roman Empire and of barbarism. Though many of them meant well, the kings were as powerless as the emperors to control corruption and extortion in the administration . . . [and] to these old abuses were now added the lawless violence of the barbarian tribesmen and of Romans who aped their manners. King Theodoric . . . had solemnly to instruct his Gothic warriors not to plunder the countryside when they [visited] Ravenna.[119]

What is more, many other parts of Europe were considerably less secure and hospitable than Italy. For example, the sixth-century chronicler Gregory of Tours told of widespread lawlessness and brutality, made worse by severe bouts of famine and plague, in Gaul, then occupied by the Franks.[120]

Attempts to Reclaim the West

The fact that barbarian rule in the west was generally incoherent and unstable was not lost on the eastern Roman emperors in Constantinople, who saw themselves as the rightful heirs to what was left of the western Empire. For a while, they maintained an uneasy truce with Odoacer, Theodoric, and other Germanic rulers. The emperor Justin I (reigned 518–527) even extended halfhearted recognition to Theodoric's regime. But this was mainly because Justin was not prepared to make the huge commitment of troops and supplies that would have been needed to reclaim the west by force.

However, Justin's successor, Justinian I (reigned 527–565), apparently felt prepared to do just that. In 533, led by the capable general Belisarius, Justinian's forces attacked and defeated the Vandal kingdom that then held sway in the former Roman province of Africa. Like the Huns before them, the once fearsome Vandals now vanished from history's stage, leaving barely a trace. Next, in 535, Belisarius invaded Ostrogothic Italy. But there he found his task a good deal harder, partly because his army was smaller than the one he had employed in Africa. Also, as Charles Freeman points out, "the Ostrogoths were resilient, while the local population was ambivalent about being rescued

by Greek-speaking easterners."[121] For these reasons, the war dragged on for some twenty years before another of Justinian's generals, Narses, managed to reconquer Rome, Ravenna, and other parts of Italy.

Yet in the end, the east's expenditure of precious time, lives, and resources came to nothing, for it failed to rebuild and revitalize the regions it had reclaimed. Through constant warfare and neglect, most of Italy had by now lost most vestiges of civil and social organization; the senatorial class had disappeared; the city of Rome's population had shrunk from its fourth-century level of perhaps eight hundred thousand to twenty-five thousand at

Justinian is often called the last true Roman emperor, mainly in reference to his ambitious dream of reconquering the lost western Roman lands and ruling over a reunited Roman Empire.

most; and poverty and misery were rampant.[122] In fact, the eastern Empire's control over Italy and Africa proved weak and relatively brief. In 568 another tribal people, the Lombards, descended into and captured most of northern and central Italy, and in the following century Muslim armies swept through northern Africa, ending Constantinople's influence in that region. Thereafter, eastern Rome, in the form of the Byzantine Empire, more or less lost contact with the west. The Byzantine rulers continued to control parts of Greece and Asia Minor, a realm that grew progressively smaller until finally falling to the Ottoman Turks in 1453.

Rome as an Idea

In spite of the upheavals and devastation that had wracked Italy and other sections of Europe in the fifth and sixth centuries, western Rome was far from dead and forgotten. Only its formal political and social apparatus had disappeared, whereas many of its cultural ideas and institutions survived to exert an enormous impact on later European civilization. The medieval kingdoms that inherited and built on Rome's wreckage absorbed these cultural elements and passed them on to the modern Western world, which is heavily indebted to the legacy of ancient Rome. As Solomon Katz states it:

> Roman civilization as a whole was greatly altered, but it survived the crises of the Later Empire and lived on as an integral element of medieval and modern civilization. Rome's triumphs and successes were canceled by her [ultimate political] failure, but what

she accomplished in diverse areas of endeavor was not lost. In the long perspective of history the survival of Roman civilization, the heritage which generation after generation has accepted, is perhaps more significant than the decline of Rome.[123]

Among the most significant aspects of that heritage are elements of Roman law, language, and religion. European law courts adopted the concepts of trial by jury, impartial justice, and unwritten "laws of nature" from Roman law. And the Justinian Code, a massive sixth-century compilation of Roman statutes and commentaries on them, profoundly influenced European justice systems, including those of the Germans, Dutch, French, and modern South Africans (who inherited their system from the Dutch). No less influential was the means of expressing these laws. Adapted by diverse peoples, Latin gradually developed into the so-called Romance languages—French, Spanish, Portuguese, Italian, and Romanian—and the Germanic tongues of the Angles and Saxons mixed with Latin and French to form English, half the words of which are of Latin origin. Moreover, Latin survived as the leading language of European scholars, as well as the official language of the Roman Catholic Church. As the ancient world transformed into the medieval, that church, which had risen to dominate Rome in its final two centuries, became the chief unifying force of European civilization, influencing and shaping daily life and thought.

To these profound legacies can be added many other modern institutions and concepts originated by the Romans (or adopted by them from the Greeks,

A section from Justinian's pandects, or complete legal codes, which had a profound effect on the later development of European law. The original achievement had three parts: the Code, a compilation of existing laws and imperial decrees; the Digest, a collection of eminent jurists' interpretations of these laws; and the Institutes, a textbook for law students.

Persians, Egyptians, or others). Anthony Kamm offers a partial list:

> Banking, public hospitals, the postal system, the daily newspaper, the fire service, central heating, glass windows, apartment buildings, sanitation, drainage, and sewers, social [welfare] benefits, and public education are all Roman institutions. So is that universal common bond and basis of social life throughout the modern world, which they called *familia* (the household) and we recognize as the . . . family unit.[124]

In a very real way, then, Rome never fell, but merely passed from the world of flesh and blood into the domain of thoughts and ideas, where it will no doubt remain alive and well for untold ages to come. And in this sense, the old Roman adage of *Roma aeterna,* "eternal Rome," has become a living truth.

Appendix

Emperors of Imperial Rome from Augustus to Justinian I

Pax Romana

Augustus, reigned 27 B.C.–A.D. 14
Tiberius, A.D. 14–37
Caligula, 37–41
Claudius, 41–54
Nero, 51–68
Galba, Otho, Vitellius, Vespasian, 69 ("year of the four emperors")
Vespasian, 69–79
Titus, 79–81
Domitian, 81–96
Nerva, 96–98
Trajan, 98–117
Hadrian 117–138
Antoninus Pius, 138–161
Marcus Aurelius, 161–180

Transition from *Pax Romana* to "Century of Crisis"

Commodus, 180–192
Pertinax, Didius Julianus, 193

Severan Dynasty

Septimius Severus, 193–211
Caracalla, 211–217
Macrinus, 217–218
Elagabalus, 218–222
Alexander Severus, 222–235

Anarchy

Maximinus, 235–238
Gordian I, Gordian II, Balbinus, Pupienus, 238
Gordian III, 238–244
Philip the "Arab," 244–249
Decius, 249–251
Gallus, 251–253
Aemilianus, 253
Valerian, 253–260
Gallienus (Valerian's son and co-emperor), 253–268
Claudius II "Gothicus," 268–270
Quintillus, 270
Aurelian, 270–275
Tacitus, 276
Florianus, 276
Probus, 276–282
Carus, 282–283
Carinus and Numerian (sons of Carus and co-emperors), 283–284

"Later Empire" Initiated by Diocletian

West		East
	First Tetrarchy	
Maximian (Augustus), 285–305		Diocletian (Augustus), 284–305
Constantius (Caesar), 293–305		Galerius (Caesar), 293–305
	Second Tetrarchy	
Constantius (Augustus), 305–306		Galerius (Augustus), 305–311
Severus (Caesar), 305–306		Maximin (Caesar), 305–308
	Civil Wars	
Severus, 306–307		Maximin, 308–313
Constantine I, 307–324		Licinius, 308–324
	Constantine I, sole ruler 324–337	
Constantine II, 337–340		Constantius II, 337–350
Constans, 340–350		
	Constantius II, sole ruler 350–361	
	Julian, sole ruler 361–363	
	Jovian, sole ruler 363–364	
Valentinian I, 364–365		Valens, 364–378
Gratian, 367–383		Theodosius I, 379–392
Valentinian II, 383–392		
	Theodosius I, sole ruler 392–395	
Honorius, 395–423		Arcadius, 395–408
Constantius III, 423		Theodosius II, 408–450
John, 423–425		
Valentinian III, 425–455		Marcian, 450–457
Petronius Maximus, 455		
Avitus, 455–456		
Majorian, 457–461		Leo I, 457–474
Libius Severus, 461–465		
Anthemius, 467–472		
Olybrius, 472		
Glycerius, 473		
Julius Nepos, 473–475		Leo II, 474
Romulus Augustulus, 475–476		Zeno, 474–491
(western throne hereafter vacant)		Anastasius I, 491–518
		Justin I, 518–527
		Justinian I, 527–565
		(eastern throne continues to be occupied until 1453)

Notes

Introduction: Descent into the Kingdom of Rust

1. *Anonymous Valesianus,* quoted in J. B. Bury, *History of the Later Roman Empire, 395–565,* vol. 1. New York: Dover, 1957, p. 406.

2. Mortimer Chambers, introduction to Mortimer Chambers, ed., *The Fall of the Roman Empire: Can It Be Explained?* New York: Holt, Rinehart, and Winston, 1963, p. 1.

3. Chambers, *The Fall of the Roman Empire,* p. 1.

4. Solomon Katz, *The Decline of Rome and the Rise of Medieval Europe.* Ithaca, NY: Cornell University Press, 1955, p. 74.

5. Edward Gibbon, *The Decline and Fall of the Roman Empire.* 3 vols. Ed. David Womersley. New York: Penguin, 1994, vol. 2, p. 512.

6. Bury, *Later Roman Empire,* vol. 1, p. 311. Following this reasoning, Bury added, "It may be said that a German penetration of western Europe must ultimately have come about. But even if that were certain, it might have happened in another way, at a later time, more gradually, and with less violence" (p. 313).

7. Averil Cameron, *The Later Roman Empire: A.D. 284–430.* Cambridge, MA: Harvard University Press, 1993, p. 12.

8. Dio Cassius, *Roman History,* quoted in Stewart Perowne, *The End of the Roman World.* New York: Thomas Y. Crowell, 1966, p. 14.

Chapter 1: From Obscurity to Mediterranean Mastery: Rome's Rise to Greatness

9. Anthony Kamm, *The Romans: An Introduction.* London: Routledge, 1995, p. 2.

10. T. J. Cornell, *The Beginnings of Rome.* London: Routledge, 1995, p. 81.

11. Livy, *The History of Rome from Its Foundation.* Books 1–5 published as *Livy: The Early History of Rome,* trans. Aubrey de Sélincourt. New York: Penguin, 1971, p. 95.

12. Livy, *The Early History of Rome,* p. 101.

13. Cicero, *Laws,* in Naphtali Lewis and Meyer Reinhold, eds., *Roman Civilization, Sourcebook 1: The Republic.* New York: Harper and Row, 1966, p. 380.

14. Cicero, *Pro Cluentio,* quoted in Michael Grant, *The World of Rome.* New York: New American Library, 1960, p. 100.

15. Michael Grant, *History of Rome.* New York: Scribner's, 1978, pp. 65–66.

16. Cicero, *Laws,* in *On the Republic and On the Laws,* trans. Clinton W. Keyes. Cambridge, MA: Harvard University Press, 1966, pp. 375–77.

17. The term "Punic" was derived from the Latin word *Punicus,* meaning Phoenician, the name of the Near Eastern maritime/trading people who originally founded Carthage in about 850 B.C.

18. Appian, *Civil Wars,* in Lewis and Reinhold, *Sourcebook 1,* p. 305.

19. Notable exceptions were the third emperor, Caligula, Augustus's great-grandson (reigned A.D. 37–41); the fifth emperor, Nero, Augustus's great-great-grandson (reigned 51–68); and Domitian, last ruler of the Flavian dynasty (reigned 81–96). All three earned reputations for demented and/or cruel behavior and met violent ends, Caligula and Domitian by assassination, and Nero by his own hand after being declared an "enemy of the people."

20. Gibbon, *Decline and Fall,* vol. 1, pp. 101–3.

21. Aelius Aristides, *Roman Panegyric,* in Naphtali Lewis and Meyer Reinhold, eds., *Roman Civilization, Sourcebook 2: The Empire.* New York: Harper and Row, 1966, p. 138.

Chapter 2: To the Brink and Back: Weathering the Century of Crisis

22. For some four hundred years, much of the Near East lying beyond the Roman provinces in Asia Minor and Palestine had been under the control of the Parthian Empire. In A.D. 226, the last Parthian king, Artabanus V, was overthrown by Ardashir, who hailed from Fars on the northern shore of the Persian Gulf, the region that had been the heartland of the old Persian Empire, which the Greek conqueror Alexander the Great had destroyed in the 320s B.C. Proclaiming himself heir to old Persia, Ardashir established the Sassanian realm, which revived Persian religion and customs and adopted a policy of expelling foreigners, including the Romans, from much of the Near East.

23. Chester G. Starr, *A History of the Ancient World.* New York: Oxford University Press, 1991, p. 653.

24. Charles Freeman, *Egypt, Greece, and Rome: Civilizations of the Ancient Mediterranean.* Oxford: Oxford University Press, 1996, p. 463.

25. The Danube River, flowing roughly west to east across central Europe, had long separated "civilized" Roman lands from the wilds of the "barbarian" north. The provinces of (west to east) Rhaetia, Noricum, Pannonia, Dacia, and Moesia bordered the northern frontier. The buffer zone they created between the barbarians and the Roman heartland was surprisingly narrow; northern Italy lay less than two hundred miles south of the Danube in Rhaetia and Noricum.

26. Dio Cassius, *Roman History,* quoted in Chris Scarre, *Chronicle of the Roman Emperors.* New York: Thames and Hudson, 1995, p. 118.

27. *Augustan History,* published as *Lives of the Later Caesars, the First Part of the* Augustan History, *with Newly Compiled* Lives *of Nerva and Trajan,* trans. Anthony Birley. New York: Penguin, 1976, pp. 163, 165–66.

28. More and more small farmers, unable to compete with the *latifundia,* large farming estates owned by wealthy Romans or the state, abandoned their fields. A number of these plots remained unused for decades or even centuries. Desperate, some of the newly landless migrated to the cities in search of work; others ended up as *coloni,* low-paid tenants on the larger farms.

29. Quoted in Dio Cassius, *Roman History,* published as *Dio's History of Rome and Annals of the Roman People,* trans. Herbert B. Foster, 6 vols., Troy, NY: Pafraets, 1906, p. 387; also see E. Cary's major translation of this work for the Loeb Classical Library (Cambridge, MA: Harvard University Press, 1927, 77.15.2).

30. Actually, both Caracalla and Geta succeeded their father and bore the imperial title of Augustus; however, less than ten months later, the ambitious Caracalla murdered his brother, who was a year younger.

31. Scarre, *Chronicle of the Roman Emperors,* p. 169.

32. When Valerian died, Shapur had his skin removed, dyed red, and hung in a Persian temple as a grisly reminder to visiting Roman delegations of Sassanian power and determination.

33. Herodian, *History,* quoted in Lewis and Reinhold, *Sourcebook 2,* pp. 437–38.

34. Starr, *Ancient World,* p. 653.

35. A. H. M. Jones, *Constantine and the Conversion of Europe.* Toronto: University of Toronto Press, 1978, pp. 19–21.

36. Michael Grant, *The Fall of the Roman Empire.* New York: Macmillan, 1990, p. 3.

37. Edward Gibbon admired Zenobia as one of the ancient world's most heroic and noble women. For his detailed and masterfully

worded account of her exploits, see *Decline and Fall,* vol. 1, pp. 312–21.

Chapter 3: Order and Security Restored: Diocletian Reorganizes the Empire

38. Cameron, *Later Roman Empire,* p. 46.

39. Some scholars point out that Diocletian probably did not initiate all of these measures, that some of his immediate predecessors, notably the emperor Aurelian, had already taken some steps in this direction. Thus, it would be more accurate to regard Diocletian's eastern-style court as the culmination or mature development of an ongoing trend.

40. Jones, *Constantine and the Conversion of Europe,* pp. 26–27.

41. Cameron, *Later Roman Empire,* p. 39.

42. *Life of Carus,* in *Augustan History,* quoted in Cameron, *Later Roman Empire,* p. 32.

43. Aurelius Victor, *Lives of the Emperors,* quoted in Lewis and Reinhold, *Sourcebook 2,* p. 457.

44. Victor, *Lives,* quoted in Lewis and Reinhold, *Sourcebook 2,* p. 457.

45. Allectus had recently murdered his mentor, Marcus Carausius, another distinguished military general turned usurper. In 287 Carausius had seized control of Britain, declaring himself independent of imperial authority, and in the next five years he incorporated parts of Gaul into his domain and even issued his own coins.

46. A. H. M. Jones, *The Later Roman Empire, 284–602.* 1964. Reprinted, Norman: University of Oklahoma Press, 1975, p. 687.

47. Arther Ferrill, *The Fall of the Roman Empire: The Military Explanation.* New York: Thames and Hudson, 1986, p. 45.

48. Lesley Adkins and Roy A. Adkins, *Handbook to Life in Ancient Rome.* New York: Facts On File, 1994, p. 54. The exact nature and chronology of Rome's frontier forts and mobile armies is still a matter of debate among historians. Among the major works advocating the defense-in-depth strategy are E. N. Luttwak, *The Grand Strategy of the Roman Empire from the First Century A.D. to the Third.* Baltimore: Johns Hopkins University Press, 1977; and A. Ferrill, *The Fall of the Roman Empire: The Military Explanation* (see note 47). In contrast, some scholars argue that archaeological evidence supporting a defense-in-depth is scanty, that such a strategy never took hold in the Empire's eastern sector, and that the *limitanei* developed after rather than during Constantine's time. See A. Cameron, *Later Roman Empire,* pp. 141–43, and B. Isaac, *The Limits of Empire: The Roman Army in the East.* Oxford: Clarendon Press, 1992, chapter 4.

49. The largest single imperial army on record—some sixty-five thousand troops—was fielded by the emperor Julian in 363 for a campaign against Persia.

50. Perowne, *The End of the Roman World,* p. 21.

51. Diocletian, *Economic Edict,* in Paul J. Alexander, ed., *The Ancient World: To 300 A.D.* New York: Macmillan, 1963, pp. 310–12; a more detailed transcription appears in Lewis and Reinhold, *Sourcebook 2,* pp. 464–72.

52. Lactantius, *The Deaths of the Persecutors,* quoted in Jones, *Constantine and the Conversion of Europe,* p. 32.

53. From the *Theodosian Code,* quoted in Lewis and Reinhold, *Sourcebook 2,* p. 482.

54. From the *Theodosian Code,* quoted in Lewis and Reinhold, *Sourcebook 2,* p. 483.

55. See Lewis and Reinhold, *Sourcebook 2,* pp. 479–81, for transcriptions of various fourth-century laws regarding the *decurions* and their burdens.

56. Jones, *Constantine and the Conversion of Europe,* pp. 32–33.

Chapter 4: "Conquer by This": Constantine and the Triumph of Christianity

57. L. P. Wilkinson, *The Roman Experience.* Lanham, MD: University Press of America, 1974, p. 196.

58. Although the troops proclaimed Constantine Augustus on July 25, 306, his reign is officially dated from the late summer of 307, when Maximian, resting his authority on his status as one of the Augusti of the original Tetrarchy, acknowledged the younger man's new rank in an official ceremony.

59. Eusebius, *Life of Constantine,* quoted in Stewart Perowne, *Caesars and Saints: The Rise of the Christian State,* A.D. *180–313.* 1962. Reprinted, New York: Barnes and Noble, 1992, p. 175.

60. Jones, *Constantine and the Conversion of Europe,* pp. 85–86.

61. Besides believing in various gods, the Romans took for granted the existence of magic. They also put great store in dreams, which they thought prophesied future events. Also, in ancient times gods often appeared in people's dreams and, as L. P. Wilkinson points out, "to people unaware that a person's preconceived ideas condition the content of his dreams, these appearances naturally seemed irrefutable evidence of the god's existence" (*The Roman Experience,* p. 191). This common experience may have been the basis for Eusebius's claim that Christ appeared to Constantine in a dream.

62. Freeman, *Egypt, Greece, and Rome,* p. 490.

63. Harold Mattingly, *The Man on the Roman Street.* New York: W. W. Norton, 1966, p. 56.

64. The phrase comes from the *Annals* (15.43) of the first-century Roman historian Tacitus, who cites it as one of the reasons (the other being arson) for the arrest of many Christians following the great fire that swept the city of Rome in A.D. 64.

65. Eusebius, *Ecclesiastical History,* in Lewis and Reinhold, *Sourcebook 2,* pp. 599–600.

66. Jones, *Constantine and the Conversion of Europe,* p. 86. This event may have constituted only part of his equation of the two gods. In the immediately preceding decades, many Christians had come to picture their god as a sun deity riding a chariot through the sky. Perhaps Constantine and his father knew of this and saw it as sufficient reason not to follow Diocletian's and Galerius's policy of persecution.

67. His mints turned out coins honoring "Hercules the Victorious," "Jupiter the Preserver," and other traditional gods at least until 317, and coins dedicated to the Unconquered Sun until 320 or 321.

68. Quoted in Jones, *Constantine and the Conversion of Europe,* p. 83.

69. Edict of Milan, in Eusebius, *Ecclesiastical History,* 2 vols., trans. Roy J. Deferrari. Washington, DC: Catholic University of America Press, 1955, vol. 1, p. 269.

70. Jones, *Constantine and the Conversion of Europe,* pp. 202–203.

71. This did not end the controversy, however; Donatists continued to flourish on the fringes of the faith until the church condemned them as heretics in the early 400s.

72. Michael Grant, *Constantine the Great: The Man and His Times.* New York: Scribner's, 1994, p. 168.

73. Cameron, *Later Roman Empire,* p. 59.

74. Ammianus Marcellinus, *History,* published as *The Later Roman Empire,* A.D. *354–378,* trans. and ed. Walter Hamilton. New York: Penguin Books, 1986, pp. 295–96.

75. Some temples were demolished, others turned into museums, and still others transformed into Christian churches.

76. Gibbon, *Decline and Fall,* vol. 1, p. 725.

Chapter 5: A Society in Transition: Life and Culture in the Later Empire

77. A. H. M. Jones, *The Decline of the Ancient World*. London: Longman Group, 1966, pp. 360–61.

78. *Latin Panegyrics,* quoted in Lewis and Reinhold, *Sourcebook 2*, p. 478.

79. Michael Grant, *A Social History of Greece and Rome*. New York: Scribner's Sons, 1992, pp. 90–91.

80. *Justinian Code* (11.52.1), quoted in Jones, *Decline*, p. 293.

81. Mattingly, *The Man on the Roman Street*, p. 147.

82. Ammianus, *Later Roman Empire*, p. 345.

83. Symmachus, *Letters*, quoted in J. P. V. D. Balsdon, *Life and Leisure in Ancient Rome*. New York: McGraw-Hill, 1969, p. 220.

84. Although a devout Christian, Sidonius wrote mostly secular works.

85. Symmachus, *On the Altar of Victory*, in Brian Tierney, ed., *The Middle Ages, vol. 1, Sources of Medieval History*. New York: Knopf, 1973, p. 24.

86. Ambrose, *"Letter to Valentinian II,"* in Tierney, *The Middle Ages*, p. 26.

87. This was at least the official arrangement; common practice was often quite different. Mixed bathing was introduced in the first century A.D. but banned again in the second century. Flagrant violations continued into the Later Empire, as evidenced by Ammianus's reference to mixed bathing *(History,* 28.4.9).

88. Teams of horses were also provided by wealthy individuals; Symmachus was an outstanding example in the Later Empire.

89. Ammianus, *Later Roman Empire*, p. 361.

90. Jones, *Decline*, p. 331.

91. Tertullian, *Apology*, quoted in Peter Quennell, *The Colosseum*. New York: Newsweek Book Division, 1971, p. 75.

92. Freeman, *Egypt, Greece, and Rome*, p. 517.

93. These restrictions were observed mainly in the west. In the east, the emperor Theodosius II restored the old divorce laws between 439 and 449; there, a woman could once again divorce her husband at will, although if she cited no specific reason she had to wait five years before remarrying.

94. Cameron, *Later Roman Empire*, pp. 126–27.

95. *Theodosian Code,* quoted in Lewis and Reinhold, *Sourcebook 2*, p. 487.

96. Grant, *World of Rome*, p. 320.

Chapter 6: Into the Realm of Legend: The Fall of the Western Empire

97. André Piganiol, "The Causes of the Ruin of the Roman Empire," in Donald Kagan, ed., *Decline and Fall of the Roman Empire: Why Did It Collapse?* Boston: D. C. Heath, 1962, p. 91.

98. Ferrill, *Fall*, pp. 164–69.

99. Piganiol, "Causes," in Kagan, *Decline and Fall*, p. 90.

100. Tacitus, *Germania*, in H. Mattingly, trans., *Tacitus on Britain and Germany*. Baltimore: Penguin, 1954, pp. 104–106.

101. Perowne, *The End of the Roman World*, p. 42.

102. Ferrill, *Fall*, pp. 84–85, 140.

103. Ferrill, *Fall*, p. 50.

104. Grant, *Fall*, p. 38.

105. Ammianus, *Later Roman Empire*, pp. 411–12.

106. The number of Romans killed at Adrianople is uncertain; modern estimates range from ten thousand to forty thousand. Even the more conservative figure represents a military disaster for Rome, since the casualties were among its best-trained troops, and recruiting, equipping, and training their replacements was an immensely difficult and expensive endeavor.

107. Quoted in Michael Grant, *The Roman Emperors*. New York: Barnes and Noble, 1997, p. 264.

108. Freeman, *Egypt, Greece, and Rome,* p. 507.

109. Honorius at first held court in Milan, but in 402 he moved his capital to Ravenna on the northeastern Italian coast, a city surrounded by marshes and therefore less vulnerable to enemy attack.

110. Peter Heather, *The Goths.* Cambridge, MA: Blackwell, 1996, p. 148.

111. Jerome, *Letter 127,* in Leon Bernard and Theodore B. Hodges, eds., *Readings in European History.* New York: Macmillan, 1958, p. 44; also see the fine translation in F. A. Wright, trans., *Select Letters of St. Jerome.* Cambridge, MA: Harvard University Press, 1963, p. 463.

112. Bury, *Later Roman Empire,* vol. 1, p. 296.

113. Jones, *Decline,* p. 362.

114. Freeman, *Egypt, Greece, and Rome,* p. 525.

Epilogue: The Living Legacy of Rome

115. Ferdinand Lot, *The End of the Ancient World and the Beginnings of the Middle Ages.* New York: Harper and Row, 1961, pp. 237, 239.

116. Theodoric also erected new buildings, including a palace and a church dedicated to St. Martin, both in Ravenna. Only a single wall of the palace survives today, but some of the original mosaics of the church, now called San Apollinare Nuovo, have been preserved.

117. Theodoric reserved most of the military offices for Goths, but this upset no one, since most army leaders in prior decades had been barbarians anyway. He called his field generals *comites,* or counts, and *duces,* or dukes, traditional military titles of the Later Empire, which, over time, were adopted by medieval lords.

118. Procopius, *The Gothic Wars,* quoted in Perowne, *End of the Roman World,* p. 102.

119. Jones, *Decline,* p. 102.

120. See Gregory of Tours, *A History of the Franks.* trans. O. M. Dalton. 2 vols. Oxford: Clarendon Press, 1927.

121. Freeman, *Egypt, Greece, and Rome,* p. 546.

122. Historians Tim Cornell and John Matthews point out the irony of the east's botched efforts to rescue its fellow Romans in the west: "As for Rome and Italy . . . their latest period of prosperity, under the favorable eye of Germanic kings, was ended by a Byzantine court's repossession of them as impoverished provinces of a Roman Empire now governed from Constantinople" (*Atlas of the Roman World.* New York: Facts On File, 1982, p. 223).

123. Katz, *Decline,* p. 139.

124. Kamm, *The Romans,* p. 201.

For Further Reading

Isaac Asimov, *The Roman Empire*. Boston: Houghton Mifflin, 1967. An excellent overview of the main events of the Empire; so precise and clearly written that even very basic readers will benefit.

Lionel Casson, *Everyday Life in Ancient Rome*. New York: American Heritage, 1975. A fine presentation of how the Romans lived: their homes, streets, entertainments, eating habits, theaters, religion, slaves, marriage customs, government, tombstone epitaphs, and more. Aimed at intermediate and advanced readers.

Jill Hughes, *Imperial Rome*. New York: Gloucester Press, 1985. This nicely illustrated introduction to the Roman Empire is aimed at basic readers.

Anthony Marks and Graham Tingay, *The Romans*. London: Usborne, 1990. An excellent summary of the main aspects of Roman history, life, and arts, supported by hundreds of beautiful and accurate drawings reconstructing Roman times. Aimed at basic readers but highly recommended for anyone interested in Roman civilization.

Don Nardo, *The Roman Empire*. San Diego: Lucent Books, 1994. A concise overview of Roman personalities and events from the rise of Augustus through the Empire's fall to the barbarians.

———, *The Fall of the Roman Empire*. San Diego: Greenhaven Press, 1997. This collection of essays, each advocating a specific cause for the fall of the western Empire, is very useful as a companion to this historical overview of Rome's last few centuries. Both books are aimed at junior high and high school readers, but their scholarly format makes them suitable for adults as well.

———, *Life in Ancient Rome*. San Diego: Lucent Books, 1997. This volume explores Roman customs, habits, beliefs, and institutions in considerable detail and includes an extensive glossary of Latin and other relevant terms.

Chester G. Starr, *The Ancient Romans*. New York: Oxford University Press, 1971. A clearly written survey of Roman history, featuring several interesting sidebars on such subjects as the Etruscans, Roman law, and the Roman army. Also contains many primary source quotes by Roman and Greek writers. For intermediate and advanced readers.

Major Works Consulted

Ancient Sources

Paul J. Alexander, ed., *The Ancient World: To 300 A.D.* New York: Macmillan, 1963. This collection of ancient writings contains several from Roman times, including Diocletian's price edict and Cyprian's description of the Christian persecutions.

Ammianus Marcellinus, *History,* published as *The Later Roman Empire, A.D. 354–378.* Trans. and ed. Walter Hamilton. New York: Penguin Books, 1986. Ammianus is now considered the finest Latin historian produced in the Later Roman Empire. His honesty, balanced judgment, and elegant writing style rank him with the likes of Livy and Tacitus, the latter to whom he is often compared. Unfortunately, only a few sections of Ammianus's history of Rome have survived, specifically those covering the years 353–378.

Appian, *Roman History.* Trans. Horace White. Cambridge, MA: Harvard University Press, 1964. Appian, a second-century A.D. Romanized Greek scholar, wrote a history of Rome from about 135 to 35 B.C. Books 13–17 of the work are commonly referred to or published separately as the *Civil Wars,* covering in some detail the strife of the first century B.C. and the fall of the Republic.

Augustan History, published as *Lives of the Later Caesars, the First Part of the* Augustan History, *with Newly Compiled* Lives *of Nerva and Trajan.* Trans. Anthony Birley. New York: Penguin, 1976. This volume contains roughly the first half of the famous history covering the lives of the emperors from Nerva to Elagabalus. Supposedly the work was compiled by six authors, but modern scholars now agree that it was written by one man pretending to be six men. His identity remains unknown. Although the work contains a considerable amount of hearsay, exaggeration, and fabrication, much of its core is factual; in any case, it remains, after Dio Cassius's history, which covers events up to A.D. 229, one of the only surviving sources covering much of the turbulent third century.

Nels M. Bailkey, ed., *Readings in Ancient History: From Gilgamesh to Diocletian.* Lexington, MA: D. C. Heath, 1976. A collection of primary source documents, including writings of Tacitus, Marcus Aurelius, Apuleius, St. Paul, Tertullian, and St. Augustine.

Leon Bernard and Theodore B. Hodges, eds., *Readings in European History.* New York: Macmillan, 1958. This collection of ancient, medieval, and modern writings includes excerpts from the works of Dio Cassius, Tacitus, Pliny the Younger, Eusebius, Ammianus, St. Jerome, Sidonius, and others dealing with the Roman Empire.

Cicero, *On the Republic and On the Laws.* Trans. Clinton W. Keyes. Cambridge, MA: Harvard University Press, 1966. In the *Laws,* the great republican champion describes the various state offices, including those of consul, censor, aedile, praetor, and dictator.

Dio Cassius, *Roman History.* Trans. E. Cary. Cambridge, MA: Harvard University Press, 1927. An excellent modern translation of Dio's important work about the events of Augustus Caesar's rise to power and reign as the first Roman emperor.

J. Wight Duff and Arnold M. Duff, trans., *Minor Latin Poets.* Cambridge, MA: Harvard University Press, 1968. Among the pieces presented here is the *Voyage Home to Gaul* of the late Roman poet Rutilius Namatianus. Part of this work is a glowing tribute to Roman glory that has often been called "Rome's swan song."

Eusebius, *Ecclesiastical History.* 2 vols. Trans. Roy J. Deferrari. Washington, DC: Catholic University of America Press, 1955. This chronicle of the struggles of the early Christians by Eusebius, one of the most important of the early church fathers (who also wrote a biography of the emperor Constantine), contains descriptions of several Christian persecutions, as well as a transcription of the famous Edict of Milan.

Jerome, *Letters,* excerpted in F. A. Wright, trans., *Select Letters of St. Jerome.* Cambridge, MA: Harvard University Press, 1963. Of main interest here is *Letter 127,* which contains the emotional reaction of this important early Christian writer on hearing of the A.D. 410 sack of Rome by the Visigoths.

Lactantius, *The Deaths of the Persecutors,* in Sister Mary Francis McDonald, trans., *Lactantius: Minor Works.* Washington, DC: Catholic University of America Press, 1965. This work by the early Christian apologist Lactantius, whose formal name was Lucius Caelius Firmi-anus, contains a vivid description of the emperor Diocletian's persecution of the Christian sect.

Naphtali Lewis and Meyer Reinhold, eds., *Roman Civilization, Sourcebook 1: The Republic* and *Roman Civilization, Sourcebook 2: The Empire.* Both New York: Harper and Row, 1966. Huge, comprehensive collections of original Roman documents, from the founding of the city to its fall, including inscriptions, papyri, and government edicts, as well as formal writings by authors ranging from Livy to Cicero to St. Augustine. Also contains much useful commentary.

Livy, *The History of Rome from Its Foundation.* Books 1–5 published as *Livy: The Early History of Rome.* Trans. Aubrey de Sélincourt. New York: Penguin, 1971; books 31–45 published as *Livy: Rome and the Mediterranean.* Trans. Henry Bettenson. New York: Penguin, 1976. Excellent translations of these parts of Livy's massive and masterful history, written during Rome's golden literary age of the late first century B.C.

Plutarch, *Lives of the Noble Grecians and Romans.* Trans. John Dryden. New York: Random House, 1932. Dryden's stately translation is one of the most often quoted of the various modern versions of Plutarch, whose famous *Parallel Lives* (the original title of the work) includes biographies of Romulus, Rome's founder; Fabius Maximus, who squared off against Hannibal in the Second Punic War; and various figures from the era of the collapsing Republic, among them Sulla, Pompey, Caesar, Cicero, and Antony.

Tacitus, *Germania,* in H. Mattingly, trans., *Tacitus on Britain and Germany.* Baltimore: Penguin, 1954. This is a very fine translation of Tacitus's book describing the German tribes of his own time (late first century A.D.), and his *Agricola,* a tract about his father-in-law, who served as governor of Roman Britain.

Modern Sources

Peter Brown, *The World of Late Antiquity, A.D. 150–750.* New York: Harcourt Brace, 1971. This important and influential book emphasizes the continuity of Roman life from the fifth to the sixth century, and the gradual, rather than catastrophic, transformation of the ancient world into medieval times.

J. B. Bury, *History of the Later Roman Empire, 395–565.* 2 vols. New York: Dover, 1957. The late, great Bury (1861–1927), who taught history at Trinity College, Dublin, produced several historical works on the classical world now considered modern classics, among them his massive and still largely authoritative *History of Greece.* His even more massive *Later Roman Empire* is still consulted by historians for its impressively detailed and accurate chronology of events.

Averil Cameron, *The Later Roman Empire: A.D. 284–430.* Cambridge, MA: Harvard University Press, 1993. A concise but very well researched and insightful look at the events, figures, and forces that shaped later Roman times. Cameron takes the position, one that has become increasingly popular among historians, that the crisis of the third century was only a temporary phase in an evolving imperial system.

Tim Cornell and John Matthews, *Atlas of the Roman World.* New York: Facts On File, 1982. This very handsomely mounted volume contains hundreds of excellent photos, maps, and drawings. The text is well written and sufficiently comprehensive to warrant calling this an illustrated history rather than a mere atlas.

Arther Ferrill, *The Fall of the Roman Empire: The Military Explanation.* New York: Thames and Hudson, 1986. In this excellent work, written in a straightforward style, Ferrill builds a strong case for his supposition that Rome fell mainly because its army grew increasingly less disciplined and formidable in the Empire's last two centuries, while at the same time the overall defensive strategy of the emperors was ill conceived and contributed to the ultimate fall.

Charles Freeman, *Egypt, Greece, and Rome: Civilizations of the Ancient Mediterranean.* Oxford: Oxford University Press, 1996. Contains a very well researched, up-to-date, and clearly written general discussion of Roman history and culture.

Edward Gibbon, *The Decline and Fall of the Roman Empire.* First published 1776–1788. The major modern editions include a seven-volume version edited by the noted historian J. B. Bury (London: Methuen, 1909–1914), later published in three volumes (New York: Heritage Press, 1946) (Bury's version, which features voluminous and useful editor's notes, is the one most often used by scholars); the three-volume version edited by David Womersley (New York: Penguin, 1994); the two-volume version in *Great Books of the*

Western World (Chicago: Encyclopaedia Britannica, 1952; the print in this edition is small and difficult to read); and a one-volume abridged version edited by D. M. Low (New York: Harcourt, Brace and World, 1960). Gibbon's masterwork, with its considerable insights, uncompromising honesty, and impressive attention to detail, still overshadows the debate about Rome's fall. One can argue with Gibbon, but the greatness of his achievement is undeniable.

Michael Grant, *The Climax of Rome.* New York: New American Library, 1968. Grant, one of the most prolific and craftsmanlike of modern classical scholars, here delivers a very readable and thought-provoking study of late Roman civilization, focusing mainly on the highest levels of achievement reached in such areas as government, law, education, and literature before the ultimate fall of that civilization. The section titled "The Climax of Paganism" is particularly good.

———, *History of Rome.* New York: Scribner's, 1978. This is one of the best available general histories of Roman civilization.

———, *The Fall of the Roman Empire.* New York: Macmillan, 1990. Grant here begins with a general historical sketch of Rome's last centuries and then proceeds with his main thesis, that Rome fell because of many manifestations of disunity, among them generals turning on the state, the poor versus the rich, the bureaucrats versus the people, the pagans versus the Christians, and so forth.

———, *Constantine the Great: The Man and His Times.* New York: Scribner's, 1994.

A very fine study of Constantine, his achievements (Christianity, Constantinople, etc.), and his impact on the Roman Empire and later ages.

A. H. M. Jones, *The Decline of the Ancient World.* London: Longman Group, 1966. Note: This is a shortened version of Jones's massive and highly influential *The Later Roman Empire, 284–602.* 3 vols. 1964. Reprinted, Norman: University of Oklahoma Press, 1975. A. H. M. (Arnold Hugh Martin) Jones, who died in 1970, is still looked upon by many modern scholars as a veritable fountain of information and insight on just about every facet of Roman civilization. As in the case of Gibbon, they do not always agree with him, but invariably stand in awe of his overall knowledge and scholarship.

———, *Constantine and the Conversion of Europe.* Toronto: University of Toronto Press, 1978. An excellent general overview of Constantine's world and his influence, particularly in the area of religion.

Ferdinand Lot, *The End of the Ancient World and the Beginnings of the Middle Ages.* New York: Harper and Row, 1961. Lot, the late respected classical scholar, examines the transition from Roman to medieval worlds, emphasizing the continuity, rather than the collapse, of culture.

Ramsay MacMullen, *Roman Government's Response to Crisis: A.D. 235–337.* New Haven, CT: Yale University Press, 1976. A worthwhile overview of the crisis years following the end of the Severan dynasty and the reorganization of the Empire by Diocletian and Constantine.

Stewart Perowne, *The End of the Roman World.* New York: Thomas Y. Crowell,

1966. A commendable general overview of Roman history from Diocletian's reforms to Odoacer's removal of Romulus Augustulus from the Roman throne.

————, *Caesars and Saints: The Rise of the Christian State*, A.D. *180–313.* 1962. Reprinted, New York: Barnes and Noble, 1992. Most studies of the rise of Christianity begin in earnest with the accession of Constantine. This one starts with the death of Marcus Aurelius and ends with Constantine, making the point that by the latter's day Christianity was entrenched solidly enough to make its ultimate survival almost inevitable.

Justine Davis Randers-Pehrson, *Barbarians and Romans: The Birth Struggle of Europe,* A.D. *400–700.* Norman: University of Oklahoma Press, 1983. This is a very well researched and well written examination of the so-called barbarian peoples whose kingdoms gradually supplanted Roman territories.

Chester G. Starr, *Civilization and the Caesars.* New York: Norton, 1965. In this marvelously insightful and entertaining book, Starr, a fine, respected scholar, traces the changes in the lives and worldviews of individual Romans during the imperial centuries and emphasizes how the old pagan views gave way to Christian ones, as exemplified by the outlook of men like Augustine.

————, *The Roman Empire, 27* B.C.–A.D. *476: A Study in Survival.* New York: Oxford University Press, 1982. Another worthy volume by Starr, who here outlines the main events of later Roman history and discusses some of the theories for Rome's demise.

————, *A History of the Ancient World.* New York: Oxford University Press, 1991. Undoubtedly one of the two or three best recent general overviews of antiquity. Similar in scope to James H. Breasted's venerable warhorse, *Ancient Times* (Boston: Ginn, 1944), but more up-to-date and with excellent annotated bibliographies.

Joseph Vogt, *The Decline of Rome: The Metamorphosis of Ancient Civilization.* Trans. Janet Sondheimer. London: Weidenfeld and Nicolson, 1967. A very well written, scholarly account of Rome's last centuries and the transition to medieval times.

F. W. Walbank, *The Awful Revolution: The Decline of the Roman Empire in the West.* Toronto: University of Toronto Press, 1969. Walbank, an eminent scholar, maintains that the seeds of Rome's destruction were inherent in the very fabric of classical civilization, which was dependent on slavery and therefore incapable of major intellectual and technical progress.

Additional Works Consulted

Lesley Adkins and Roy A. Adkins, *Handbook to Life in Ancient Rome*. New York: Facts On File, 1994.

J. P. V. D. Balsdon, *Life and Leisure in Ancient Rome*. New York: McGraw-Hill, 1969.

Timothy D. Barnes, *Constantine and Eusebius*. Cambridge, MA: Harvard University Press, 1981.

Norman H. Baynes and H. St. L. B. Moss, *Byzantium: An Introduction to East Roman Civilization*. Oxford: Oxford University Press, 1961.

Arthur E. R. Boak, *A History of Rome to 565 A.D.* New York: Macmillan, 1943.

———, *Manpower Shortage and the Fall of the Roman Empire in the West*. 1955. Reprinted, Westport, CT: Greenwood Press, 1974.

Peter Brown, *The Making of Late Antiquity*. Cambridge, MA: Harvard University Press, 1978.

———, *Power and Persuasion in Late Antiquity: Towards a Christian Empire*. Madison: University of Wisconsin Press, 1992.

Matthew Bunson, *A Dictionary of the Roman Empire*. Oxford: Oxford University Press, 1991.

J. B. Bury, *Invasion of Europe by the Barbarians*. New York: Norton, 1967.

Owen Chadwick, *A History of Christianity*. New York: St. Martin's Press, 1995.

Mortimer Chambers, ed., *The Fall of the Roman Empire: Can It Be Explained?* New York: Holt, Rinehart, and Winston, 1963.

T. J. Cornell, *The Beginnings of Rome*. London: Routledge, 1995.

Donald R. Dudley, *The Civilization of Rome*. New York: New American Library, 1962.

Will Durant, *Caesar and Christ: A History of Roman Civilization and of Christianity from Their Beginnings to A.D. 325*. New York: Simon and Schuster, 1944.

M. I. Finley, *Ancient Slavery and Modern Ideology*. New York: Viking, 1980.

———, *The Ancient Economy*. Berkeley: University of California Press, 1985.

Garth Fowden, *Empire to Commonwealth: Consequences of Monotheism in Late Antiquity*. Princeton, NJ: Princeton University Press, 1993.

Tenny Frank, ed., *Economic Survey of Ancient Rome*. 5 vols. New York: Octagon, 1972.

Charles Freeman, *The World of the Romans*. New York: Oxford University Press, 1993.

Walter Goffart, *Barbarians and Romans, A.D. 418–584: The Techniques of Accommodation*. Princeton, NJ: Princeton University Press, 1980.

Michael Grant, *The World of Rome*. New York: New American Library, 1960.

———, *The Army of the Caesars*. New York: M. Evans, 1974.

———, *A Social History of Greece and Rome*. New York: Scribner's Sons, 1992.

———, *Atlas of Classical History*. New York: Oxford University Press, 1994.

———, *The Antonines*. London: Routledge, 1996.

———, *The Severans*. London: Routledge, 1996.

———, *The Roman Emperors*. New York: Barnes and Noble, 1997.

Mason Hammond, *The City in the Ancient World*. Cambridge, MA: Harvard University Press, 1972.

Alfred F. Havighurst, ed., *The Pirenne Thesis: Analysis, Criticism, and Revision*. Lexington, MA: D. C. Heath, 1969.

R. M. Haywood, *Myth of Rome's Fall*. Westport, CT: Greenwood Press, 1979.

Peter Heather, *The Goths*. Cambridge, MA: Blackwell, 1996.

Walter E. Kaegi Jr., *Byzantium and the Decline of Rome*. Princeton, NJ: Princeton University Press, 1968.

Donald Kagan, ed., *Decline and Fall of the Roman Empire: Why Did It Collapse?* Boston: D. C. Heath, 1962.

Anthony Kamm, *The Romans: An Introduction*. London: Routledge, 1995.

Solomon Katz, *The Decline of Rome and the Rise of Medieval Europe*. Ithaca, NY: Cornell University Press, 1955.

Vicki León: *Uppity Women of Ancient Times*. Berkeley: Conari Press, 1995.

Ramsay MacMullen, *Constantine*. New York: Dial Press, 1969.

———, *Corruption and the Decline of Rome*. New Haven, CT: Yale University Press, 1988.

John Matthews, *The Roman Empire of Ammianus*. Baltimore: Johns Hopkins University Press, 1989.

Harold Mattingly, *The Man on the Roman Street*. New York: W. W. Norton, 1966.

John Julius Norwich, *Byzantium: The Early Centuries*. New York: Knopf, 1989.

Jaroslav Pelikan, *The Excellent Empire: The Fall of Rome and the Triumph of the Church*. San Francisco: Harper and Row, 1987.

Peter Quennell, *The Colosseum*. New York: Newsweek Book Division, 1971.

Michael I. Rostovtzeff, *Social and Economic History of the Roman Empire*. 2 vols. Oxford: Oxford University Press, 1957.

Chris Scarre, *Chronicle of the Roman Emperors*. New York: Thames and Hudson, 1995.

Brian Tierney, ed., *The Middle Ages*. Vol. 1, *Sources of Medieval History*. New York: Knopf, 1973.

Paul Veyne, ed., *From Pagan Rome to Byzantium*. Vol. 1 of Philippe Ariès and Georges Duby, eds., *A History of Private Life*. Cambridge, MA: Harvard University Press, 1987.

Lynn White Jr., ed., *The Transformation of the Roman World: Gibbon's Problem After Two Centuries*. Berkeley: University of California Press, 1966.

L. P. Wilkinson, *The Roman Experience*. Lanham, MD: University Press of America, 1974.

Index

Picture Credits

Cover photo: Erich Lessing/Art Resource, NY

Archive Photos, 48, 50, 58, 60, 66, 86

Copyright British Museum, 68

Corbis, 28, 36, 39

Heck's Pictorial Archive of Military Science, Geography and History, Ed. J G. Heck, Dover Publications, Inc., © 1994, 16, 43

Historic Costume in Pictures, Dover Publications, Inc., © 1975, 75

Joseph Paris Picture Archive, 26, 32, 87

North Wind Picture Archives, 12, 13, 15, 21, 23, 46, 54, 62, 69, 74, 77, 80

Pictorial Archive of Decorative Renaissance Woodcuts, Jost Amman, Dover Publications, Inc., © 1968, 52

Scala/Art Resource, NY, 29

Stock Montage, Inc., 18, 89

About the Author

Classical historian and award-winning writer Don Nardo has published more than twenty books about the ancient Greek and Roman world. These include general histories, such as *The Roman Empire, The Persian Empire,* and *Philip and Alexander: The Unification of Greece;* war chronicles, such as *The Punic Wars* and *The Battle of Marathon;* cultural studies, such as *Life in Ancient Greece, Greek and Roman Theater, The Age of Augustus,* and *The Trial of Socrates;* and literary companions to the works of Homer and Sophocles. Mr. Nardo also writes screenplays and teleplays and composes music. He lives with his wife, Christine, and dog, Bud, on Cape Cod, Massachusetts.